MAKE THE ADJUSTMENT

MAKE THE ADJUSTMENT

FINDING THE COURAGE TO EMBARK ON YOUR OWN JOURNEY OF TRANSFORMATIONAL CHANGE

CHRIS MADER

MANUSCRIPTS
PRESS

COPYRIGHT © 2024 CHRIS MADER

All rights reserved.

MAKE THE ADJUSTMENT

Finding the Courage to Embark on Your Own Journey of Transformational Change

ISBN   979-8-88926-183-4 *Paperback*

979-8-88926-184-1 *Hardcover*

979-8-88926-182-7 *Ebook*

Dedication

To Mom, Dad, and my wife Melissa, thank you for your unconditional love, support, and always having my back. To our children, I hope this book reinforces the foundational lessons I've tried to teach you. Life is hard and you will continuously face adversity, but you all have the strength, courage, and skills to Make the Adjustment *throughout your lifetime to attain great outcomes. I love you all and will always be there for you.*

Table of Contents

Foreword—by Joe Matarese

THE ART OF ADJUSTMENT: NAVIGATING LIFE'S INEVITABLE SHIFTS

In a world marked by perpetual change, the only certainty is the unexpected. The journey of life is akin to navigating a ship through uncharted waters, where each turn can bring about new challenges and opportunities. This book, *Make the Adjustment*, is not merely a compilation of chapters but a mosaic of life lessons, experiences, and insights. It's a narrative about adaptability, resilience, and the unyielding pursuit of personal and professional growth.

Chris Mader's journey, from the sun-soaked baseball fields to the high-pressure environment of corporate boardrooms, serves as the canvas for this book. Each step of this odyssey has been a testament to the power of adjustments—minor tweaks and major shifts that have shaped his existence. Drawing from a rich tapestry of experiences, coupled with wisdom from mentors, peers, and his own introspective voyages, this book emerges. It's a chronicle of triumphs and tribulations, a deep dive into the raw, often uncomfortable process of self-discovery and transformation.

As you traverse these pages, you'll encounter the fundamental question of "why"—the driving force behind our actions and the architect of our destiny. You will embark on a voyage through the realms of emotional intelligence, the significance of nurturing a close-knit inner circle, the steadfast mindset to take ownership of your outcomes, and the intricate dynamics of change. Each topic is not merely a subject of discussion but a layer of understanding, a cornerstone in the edifice of self-awareness and environmental mastery.

This book is more than a collection of words; it's an invitation to a journey of transformation. It's about recognizing your innate ability to shape your destiny, to pivot when the tides of life demand, and to march forward with purpose and clarity. Through personal anecdotes, practical advice, and reflective exercises, the goal is to arm you with the tools and mindset necessary to chart your course in life's complex terrains.

Make the Adjustment is more than a phrase; it's a life philosophy. It symbolizes the essence of living—a series of calculated maneuvers, spontaneous jumps, and sometimes necessary retreats. It's about finding equilibrium, aligning your inner values with your external actions, and making choices that foster fulfillment and progress.

As you delve into the book, remember that these stories, while personal to the author and those of others mentioned, are also our stories too. They reflect the universal journey of self-improvement, adjustments, and transformation that each of us undertakes. As you turn these pages, I encourage you to reflect, question, and perhaps start rewriting your own narrative. For in the end, the true measure of our journey lies not just in the destinations we reach but in the adjustments we make along the way.

At its core, this book is a celebration of the human spirit's resilience and capacity for change. It's a reminder that no matter where we come from or what path we're on, we all have the power to adjust our sails when the winds of life shift. It's about embracing change, not as a foe to fear but as a friend to understand and harness.

As we explore the concept of "why," we delve into the depths of our motivations and desires. We unravel the intricate tapestry of our innermost drives, the forces that propel us forward, and the anchors that sometimes hold us back. This exploration is more than an academic exercise; it's a journey into the heart of what makes us tick, an opportunity to align our deepest values with our daily lives.

The chapter on emotional intelligence opens the doors to a world where understanding and managing emotions are paramount. Here, we navigate the complex landscapes of our minds, learning to decipher the language of our feelings and the messages they convey. This understanding is crucial, not only for personal well-being but also for building meaningful relationships and leading effectively.

As we venture into the realm of our inner circle, we examine the profound impact of the people we choose to surround ourselves with. This chapter is a testament to the power of selective association—the idea that the quality of our relationships can significantly influence the trajectory of our lives. It's an invitation to curate our social sphere consciously; to foster connections that uplift, inspire, and propel us toward our aspirations.

The concept of the "owner's mentality" challenges us to take charge of our lives, to be the architects of our destiny. It's about cultivating a mindset of responsibility, accountability, and proactive engagement. This chapter is a call to action, urging us to step up and own every aspect of our lives—from our decisions and actions to our successes and failures.

As we delve into the dynamics of change, we confront one of life's most daunting yet exhilarating aspects. This chapter is an exploration of our capacity to evolve, adapt, and grow. It's about understanding the nature of change, the forces that drive it, and the strategies we can employ to navigate it successfully.

Throughout the book, we intertwine theoretical concepts with practical insights, ensuring that each lesson is not only understood but also actionable. This blend of theory and practice is designed to provide a comprehensive toolkit for personal and professional growth.

In each chapter, you'll find not only narratives and theories but also exercises and reflections designed to foster a deeper understanding of the content and its application to your life. These exercises are invitations to introspection and action, pushing you to apply the concepts in real-world scenarios.

Moreover, *Make the Adjustment* goes beyond the personal. It extends into the realm of leadership and community involvement. It's about how the principles of emotional intelligence, inner circle dynamics, owner's mentality, and adaptability to change can not only transform individuals but also reshape teams, organizations, and communities. It's about the ripple effect of personal growth; how our individual transformations can inspire and catalyze change in those around us.

The journey through this book is also a journey through the various stages of Mader's own life. From the discipline and focus honed on the baseball field to the strategic thinking and resilience developed in the corporate world, each chapter draws on various aspects of these experiences. They are woven together to illustrate how the lessons learned in one arena of life can be applied in another, demonstrating the universality and interconnectedness of these principles.

This book is an invitation to embark on a journey of self-discovery and transformation. It's a guide to navigating the complexities of life with agility and purpose. Whether you're a student stepping into the world, a professional seeking to elevate your career, a leader aspiring to inspire your team, or simply someone looking to live a more fulfilled life, these pages hold valuable lessons for you.

As you read, I encourage you to keep an open mind and heart. Allow the stories, concepts, and exercises to challenge your perspectives, to inspire new thoughts, and to ignite a desire for change within you. Remember, the journey of a thousand miles begins with a single step, and sometimes, the most crucial step is the willingness to *Make the Adjustment.*

In conclusion, *Make the Adjustment* is more than a book; it's a compass for life. It's a testament to the belief that we are all capable of extraordinary things if we are willing to make the necessary adjustments along the way. As you turn these pages, I hope you find inspiration, insight, and the courage to embark on your own journey of transformation. Here's to the journey ahead—may it be one of growth, discovery, and fulfillment for you.

Introduction

If you picked up this book, you've taken the first step by identifying you'd like to make a change or an adjustment in your life or business. I commend you for it, because for many people, taking the first step is the most difficult one. Anyone who embarks on a journey of any type of change will experience some level of fear, discomfort, frustration, and more. These emotions are all normal, but I will help you manage this and ultimately overcome it.

Like you, I've had my fair share of challenges throughout my lifetime. I tell my kids all the time, "Life is hard," because it is. But I've overcome the vast majority of obstacles thrown my way and accomplished some lofty goals. There have been wins, losses, setbacks, triumphs, championships, awards, sadness, frustration—all of the experiences and emotions we humans feel. However, I've been fortunate enough in my life to figure out an algorithm for "making the adjustments" necessary to overcome almost any obstacle, both in my personal and professional life, and am honored to share these discoveries with you.

My lens on life has been predominantly experienced through professional baseball and then in boardrooms around the globe. The positive result for you, the reader, are the discoveries about what the top 1 percent of successful people, athletes, and business professionals from around the world do best. What are their attributes? How do they overcome adversity and obstacles? How do they succeed when so many other people do not?

But back to why you picked up this book… Something in your life (or in your business) isn't quite going the way you wanted it to, and you're not quite sure how you got here or how to get out of the situation you find yourself in. This book will serve as a guide to support you in all those areas and more.

My inspiration and title of the book, *Make the Adjustment*, came to me in April 2023 and is written in honor of my late college coach, Boyd Coffie. He was the head baseball coach at Rollins College for more than twenty-five years and was a legend in college and professional athletics.

I have always wanted to write this book but never made the adjustments in my life to make the time to do so—until now.

When I was a little boy, my dream was to play professional baseball. I grew up in a north suburb of Boston in a middle-income neighborhood and was obsessed with baseball. I collected baseball cards, watched Boston Red Sox games, went to baseball camps, played catch with my dad, and played Home Run Derby with my friends. I also went to the batting cages whenever I could. (Thanks, Mom, for all those quarters for the batting machine!)

After putting in the proverbial ten thousand hours of work from ages ten through seventeen, I found myself at the top of amateur baseball by being named the Massachusetts Amateur Baseball Player of the Year in 1988 as well as being nominated to the US Junior Olympic team.

As a result, many colleges and universities recruiting me were Division I powerhouses. A typical college visit had the coaches and players showing me the facilities and classrooms, and eventually we would always end up at a college party of all things. (Remember, I was only seventeen at the time.) I had fun on these visits and ultimately short listed Miami, Clemson, and Dartmouth as my top three schools to attend in the fall.

My last stop was a small, private, Division II school called Rollins College in Winter Park, Florida. I really didn't plan on going to a smaller school, but *US News & World Report* ranked the school as number one in the south for many years, and many in the Northeast coined Rollins as the "ivy league of the south," which intrigued me.

At the time, I was a cocky young kid and thought I belonged at a larger Division I program, preferably one I had been watching on ESPN at the College World Series every year. But my father convinced me to make the trip to Winter Park, even though I didn't think much of it or that I would like Rollins. So I went through the motions during the visit and honestly didn't think I would go to school there.

The head coach, Boyd Coffie, was a strong but understated gentleman from Tennessee. He was a standout basketball and baseball player at Rollins, joined the army, then played professional baseball for the Yankees. He was a legendary college baseball coach in the state of Florida for twenty-five-plus seasons. He didn't really say a whole lot, but when he spoke he commanded the room and the attention of others. He had a quiet, calm, but confident presence. And during my entire day visiting Rollins as a college recruit, "Coach" didn't seem to show much interest in me. At least, that's how it felt at the time.

I vividly remember my visit as it was an extremely hot and humid spring day in Florida, and instead of sending me to parties like all of my previous college visits, Coach handed me a pair of baseball shorts and a T-shirt and informed me that I would be "working out with the team" that day. This was exciting because I thought I'd be out on the field with some of the best Division II players in the country. I was a strong hitter and solid defensive player, and I thought I was ready for the challenge. Little did I know my cocky demeanor was about to be humbled very quickly...

Instead of playing catch, hitting batting practice, or doing baseball drills, Coach informed us we would be doing a five-mile run through Central Florida, which culminates with a body weight workout called "the bars," with pull-ups, ring rows, sit ups, and dips. We never touched a baseball, a glove, or a bat, or stepped on the field that day, and I was worn out. I came in dead last in the run and dead last in the bars workout. (I couldn't even do one pull-up!) I was sweating profusely, exhausted, embarrassed, and thinking, *There's no way I'm going to school here.*

At the end of the visit, we walked into Coach Coffie's office, and after a short chat he said he would love to see me go to school there. He gave no promises on playing time, but he thought I could start as a freshman. He referenced the VHS video tape I had sent him and said he liked my swing and that it was a "pure swing and wouldn't change a thing," which was music to my ears.

He asked if I had any questions, and I really didn't, but I felt foolish not to ask him something. Then I noticed a big wooden sign hanging behind his desk that read, "Son, Make the Adjustment." I asked him what "make the adjustment" meant, and all he said in his southern drawl was, "If you come to school here, Chris, you will find out." I got instant *chills*. He caught my attention, and I was intrigued, but I didn't know those words would one day change my life.

Walking out of the stadium with one of the senior players on the team, I asked what it was like to play for Boyd. All he could say was what an amazing coach he was, how he made them overall better athletes, baseball players, and men. This player repeated Coach Coffie's thoughts about me starting as a freshman and told me there was a fifth year catcher whom I could learn a lot from. Within a span of fifteen minutes, I went from uninterested to sold and decided to attend Rollins College in the fall.

So there I was, freshman year, September 1988, a cocky kid from Massachusetts having won a bunch of accolades at the high school level. But in college, I was just a "pup," as they called all the freshman baseball players. Wherein my first *Make the Adjustment* story began.

During a fall baseball game, the pitcher's arm angle was off, but I was the only one who could see it because of my vantage point as the catcher. When I went out to the mound to let him know, all he said was, "Go back to the plate, pup, and just catch the ball." I was stunned.

In between innings I spoke with Coach, and all he said in his southern drawl was, "Chris, you gotta 'make the adjustment' on how you speak to the seniors. You're a freshman and still need to earn their respect."

At the moment I was thinking *Earn their respect? I was the Massachusetts State Player of the Year. They need to earn my respect!* But after talking to my roommate and other teammates, I started to learn my cocky attitude wasn't well received, nor should it have been. It was up to me to "make the adjustment" with my attitude and be more humble when communicating with my teammates.

Then, as someone who always got As and Bs in high school, I found myself getting Cs and Ds for the first time in my life. In order to maintain my scholarship, I needed to pull at least a 2.0 GPA each semester to keep my scholarship, which was now in jeopardy. I went to coach to talk about it (with the giant "Son, Make the Adjustment" sign hanging behind his desk), and all he said was, "Chris, you've got to make the adjustment with your studies. I'm hearing you're going to too many parties. So, you gotta stop that, and we can find you a tutor to help you in the classes you're struggling with the most."

Again, Coach was right, it was once again up to me to make the adjustments needed to improve my grades and focus my time in the right areas.

Whenever Coach Coffie would say, "Make the adjustment," it became inspirationally irritating, because once he spoke, everything seemed so clear and obvious. It's like he had this hidden intuition. He always knew what to say and when to say it.

Which leads to what caused me to write this book. I graduated from Rollins College in 1992 then played four years in professional baseball from 1992 to 1995. After my baseball career ended, I went on to a successful career in corporate America as a business executive from 1996 to 2023. But April 7, 2023, was the exact moment I knew something had to change. I truly had to make the biggest adjustment of my life.

My phone rang at 8:30 a.m. that day. I was shocked when the founder of the company informed me I would be the first victim of a "reduction in workforce." His exact words were, "Chris, you've done nothing wrong. You did everything we asked you to do and are a great leader. But the external factors in the healthcare market forced us to make some incredibly difficult decisions, and this is strictly a financial decision in order for the company to survive. I've owned this company for more than ten years and will step back in as CEO."

And just like that… I was unemployed after less than a year with this company and twenty-seven straight years of consistent, gainful employment.

After the initial shock, I started to, as Boyd would say, make the adjustment, remembering another one of Coach Coffie's great insights: "It's not adversity that's the issue; it's how you handle the adversity that comes your way."

I took the weekend to relax and take my mind off things. But first thing Monday morning, I started calling some of my closest friends, former colleagues and bosses and asked what they thought I was best at. They all agreed I am one of the best people they know when overcoming adversity, as well as a coach and developing people professionally.

And that's the story of how one of the worst things that's ever happened in my career became the launch pad for the best thing that ever happened to me, both personally and professionally.

In my heart, I always wanted to be a coach, either for business leaders or athletes. I coached my kids in baseball, flag football, and ice hockey and loved it. Coaching (in business or professional sports) has always been my "dream job." So, in less than thirty days, I:

- Created a website;
- Opened a business bank account;
- Registered my business with the state of Massachusetts;
- Created training content, initial sales collateral, service offerings, contracts, and pricing sheets; and

- I called every successful entrepreneur I knew and asked them for advice.

And when I woke up on Tuesday, May 9, 2023, MTA Consultancy LLC was open for business with a tagline of "Make the Adjustment: join us on our mission to create better leaders and sales professionals in this world." The primary service offerings were executive coaching, leadership training, sales training, and keynote/motivational speaking.

Much of my expertise in leadership and coaching came from my experiences at Randstad Technologies (now Randstad Digital), who is the number one leader in talent and human resources services in the world. I worked there for over twenty years, and while there, Randstad invested in me in the areas of:

- Adult learning theories;
- Instructional design and organizational behavior;
- Change management;
- Emotional intelligence;
- Corporate strategy; and
- Business planning.

This training exposed me to some remarkably interesting data and statistics regarding why people resist learning and development. Mostly, they weren't willing to change. I explored what I could do as a learning and development executive to help them improve and… say it with me… "make the adjustment."

While working at Randstad, we assessed the current and future leaders in the company. At the beginning of each training session, we asked them to take a change survey. Of the more than four hundred employees in leadership, sales, and operations roles, we found most people (when asked) said they were "comfortable with change." But when we started to peel the onion back on the data and dig deeper, we found only 5 percent of people were actually "comfortable with change," 20 percent were only comfortable if they "controlled the change," and 75 percent of people were "not comfortable with change" at all.

Although our assessments suggest that most of those individuals do not like change, the fact of the matter is that all of them were constantly trying to improve. The vast majority of people in this world wake up wanting to succeed and win.

To support this, there's a great statistic from *Inc. Magazine* saying 83 percent of people are well-intentioned, are fundamentally good, want to succeed and help others.[1]

But at some point, we all hit a roadblock. Some people are able to adapt, implement change, and succeed. But not everyone does. *Why?* It's due to a number of factors.

They don't have the right plan, mindset, approach, and mostly are not willing to make the adjustments necessary to change, which is usually due to lack of self-awareness. Perhaps they are in the wrong social or work circles. Perhaps they lack a plan or structure, are afraid, or experience discomfort, which halts their progress altogether.

Additionally, most people hold themselves back due to their own negative internal self-talk. They might be afraid to fail or look foolish. Or they make excuses and blame external factors for their setbacks or why things didn't work out for them. They need to make their own adjustment, but they just don't know how to.

This book will provide you with a proven approach and formula to own your outcomes and "make the adjustments" needed in your life. Not only do I have the science to prove it, but I've also lived it—multiple times.

After leaving Rollins, Boyd Coffie enjoyed a ten-year professional baseball coaching career. But in 2006 he was diagnosed with cancer, and it was a battle he regretfully did not win. Given his incredible physical condition and mental toughness throughout his life, we all thought if anyone could beat it, it would be Boyd. But it just didn't work out that way and was a tragic loss.

Rollins held a celebration of life for Boyd on campus, and more than three hundred former players were in attendance. The last person to speak at the service was one of our former teammates and Boyd's son, Trey Coffie. Trey reminisced and told a few stories many of us had never heard. We laughed quite a bit early on, but after a while, we had tears in our eyes. Some were tears of joy, but most were tears of sadness.

Trey could tell the room was sad and the mood was heavy. Witnessing hundreds of grown men crying had to be tough for him. So, he paused, looked up from his notes, and said, "Guys, if Boyd was here right now with us, what would he say?"

And in unison, more than three hundred of us who played for Boyd said, "Son, make the adjustment." It echoed. It was like Boyd was right there with us. Chills. He was still there with *all of us.* I had always thought my relationship with Boyd was special, almost as if he didn't have this connection with anyone else. On the contrary—he had it with everyone he coached.

After reflecting on the service, I knew his message of "make the adjustment" needed to be carried on. I just didn't know how or when, until now…

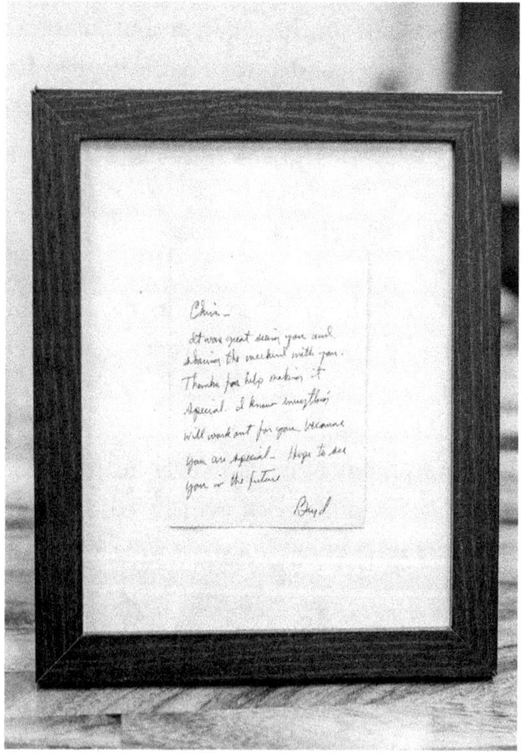

Pictured is a note from my late college baseball coach, Boyd Coffie, which sits on my desk at work.

CHAPTER 1

Why Are You Here?

Let's start by framing how this book is laid out. *Make the Adjustment* is focused on understanding and navigating change, overcoming obstacles, and attaining better outcomes. The goals you set for yourself may focus on your personal or professional growth. While anyone can leverage the content in this book, there will be breakouts in several chapters on not only implementing these concepts in your personal life but in your professional life as well.

Additionally, the end of each chapter will provide lessons for the reader entitled "Adjustments to Make." These lessons will help you stay on track and hold yourself accountable with actionable steps to apply the lessons in each chapter.

When beginning your journey of transformational change, your purpose and your "why" must be crystal clear, because you will face challenges, setbacks, and obstacles. Welcome them. Because once you know the path you are on, your mindset, deep down purpose, and your "why" will be stronger than anything that gets in your way.

The first time I heard the "why" question was while attending a leadership conference for a previous employer in 2010. Sean Brady, a C-suite business executive, calmly walked on stage, paused, and posed the following question to the 180-plus attendees, "Why are you here?"

He paused… for a while.

Then he again asked, "*Why. Are. You. Here?*"

The room was silent. We were all looking at each other. What was Sean getting at? Most of us really hadn't ever thought of "why" we were working where we were. We knew we came to work to serve our clients. We wanted to enjoy working with our colleagues. Obviously, we worked there to earn a decent living. But *why* were we there?

What he was really asking was, "What was our greater *purpose* beyond the day-to-day tasks of the job?"

After some reflection, my "why" at that time, my "intrinsic" motivation, if you will, was to be a provider for my family and to grow my career as a leader. I needed to earn a living to not only pay the bills but support my kids and give them every advantage in life I could.

But after the conference, I started to ask myself what my own greater purpose in life was beyond my career alone. I spoke with a mentor who asked me to write down how many hours there are in a month. (The answer is approximately 730.) If you subtract how many hours you sleep (240), this leaves 490 hours per month to live your best life and attain whatever goals you have.

Everyone's goals and how they spend their time will be different. But in my example, here was the list of all the important aspects of my life at the time where I needed to count the time spent in hours:

- Father
- Husband
- Son
- Friend
- Career
- Nutrition
- Physical fitness
- Hobbies
- Rest and sleep

This is a good time for you to do this same exercise. Start by defining the roles you have (or want to have) in your life:

- Career
- Significant other
- Kids
- Parents/guardians
- Siblings
- Extended family
- Current circle of friends
- Time spent on self-care (nutrition/physical fitness)
- Other hobbies or interests

- What else?
- Anything else?
- Are you sure?

Next, reflect on the past month and write down how many hours you spent within each focus area in your life?

Roles in your life	Hours per month (Current)	Hours per month (Goal)
Career		
Spouse/Partner		
Parent		
Child		
Sibling(s)		
Self Care and Hobbies		
Sleep		

Time Spent Comparison

REFLECTION POINT

Now ask yourself, "Did I achieve proper balance?" or, "Am I spending the time on the right things that will help me lead a more fulfilling life?"

If not, take a few minutes to reflect on the aspects of your life you are currently unsatisfied with and what adjustments you are willing to commit to—effective immediately.

After I completed this exercise, I then had to plan and organize time in each category to ensure I was leading a fulfilling life and not neglecting the most important aspects. When I first did this exercise, I found I was spending too much time at work and not enough time on my own self-care or with my family. My life was out of balance, and I recognized I was the one who needed to make the adjustment.

Now I am asking you this same question: Why are you here? What caused you to pick up this book? What adjustments do you want to make in your life or in your business? Because accurately answering these questions will start the snowball of actions you will be taking from this point forward.

Simon Sinek, a well-known author, and speaker, wrote one of the most impactful books on this topic called *Start with Why*. He then went on to elaborate that most people start with "what, how, and why" they do what they do. But his breakthrough concept is that the most successful people and top companies start with "why they do what they do, then the how, and then the what." He later called this concept the "Golden Circle."[1]

I couldn't agree with him more. Your "why" and your purpose has to be greater than the obstacles you will face. This is why self-awareness becomes important. Think about some of the past goals you've set for yourself that you've yet to attain. Then, be brutally honest with yourself and ask why you didn't attain the goals you intended to, or why the outcomes weren't what you had hoped for.

I'm willing to bet that when you really reflect on it, some actions you took (or didn't take) allowed these negative outcomes to occur. One of the main reasons people don't attain their goals or outcomes is they lack a greater purpose. Understanding your "why" will provide you with the boost of energy and focus needed on the days when you may not have slept well or aren't in a good mindset. Another reason people struggle to succeed is fear, which I will address later in the book.

But before we go any further, accurately answering these questions may be the most important part of this process: Why are you here, and what do you want to change?

You see, understanding your "why" and the greater purpose of whatever adjustments you are trying to make in your life is paramount to your mental state, because things will get hard. This book and lessons within are specifically here to help you navigate the obstacles thrown your way. This isn't about accomplishing someone else's goals or dreams; this is about you living the best life you can and accomplishing *your* hopes and dreams.

Yes, there will be setbacks. It won't always be easy. There will be days when you are not in a good mood. There will be naysayers, and a lot of them. But those are the days where the most successful people who accomplish great things push through the struggle and obstacles because they have the discipline, the mindset, a plan, and a greater purpose to accomplish whatever it is they have set their mind to.

When I was a young boy, I found this quote and wrote it down with a red marker on a blank piece of paper. It still sits in my old bedroom today in my parents' house and was one of the most impactful quotes I ever read: "The greatest pleasure in life is doing what others say you could not do."

Think about the most successful people you know or admire. What is the most common trait they have? Why do you think that over the long haul, they've become "successful"? What's their secret? How did they get to the top of their chosen field and attain their goals? Let's start with a list of extraordinarily successful people in multiple walks of life:

- Steve Jobs
- Kobe Bryant
- Warren Buffett
- Taylor Swift
- Tom Brady
- Albert Einstein
- Oprah Winfrey
- Bill Gates

We can list several competencies about what made these people successful. Sure, they all had drive, work ethic, relentless persistence, and so many other great attributes. But if you had to narrow it down to just *one*, what would it be? Let's explore that and see what they had to say.

In 2023, after his retirement from professional football, Tom Brady (seven-time Super Bowl champion as an NFL quarterback) said, "It wasn't my goal to be the 'greatest of all time.' I was motivated to be the best that I could be and to do the best with the opportunities that I had."[2] Sure, he was aware of the records and those who came before him, but he measured himself against himself.

Steve Jobs believed, "You have to love what you do, because the only way to do (anything great) is to love to do what you do."[3] Apple's tagline at one point was "Think Different," which was to say they didn't want to be like anyone else, they wanted to be a company with unique products and services. Again, they were aware what their competitors were up to, but they were forging their own path and building the products and services they knew people would love.

One of the NBA's all-time greats Kobe Bryant once defined something he called the "Mamba mentality," which means he was "just trying to get better every day. It's the simplest form of just trying to get better at whatever it is that you're doing."[4] Yes, Kobe may have had some incredible athletic ability, but he wanted to master every nuance of the sport of basketball that he could.

Taylor Swift is now challenging The Beatles for the most albums ever sold. She once said, "I don't compare myself to anyone else."[5] Clearly, she is doing something right and dominating the music industry with a net worth exceeding $1.1 billion by the age of thirty-three.[6]

As you read through what these people said and subsequently accomplished, it's clear the greats were all very clear on their *why* and their *purpose*. They had a growth mindset, sought to continuously improve, and loved what they did.

After studying these greats, really listening to what they say and subsequently do, we realize they have many traits in common. The most successful people compare themselves to themselves; they play a game of me versus me. Yes, they are aware of those who came before them and who their competition is, but they understand that each individual or team has a unique set of circumstances, strengths, and weaknesses that others may not have. When it comes to attaining their goals, improving, and getting continuously better in their chosen field, brutal honesty and authenticity are key.

The greats know who they are and are comfortable with themselves. They are less focused on other people and more focused on what they say and do. Their style, opinions, the way they treat others, relationships… everything is unique. They are not trying to be like everyone else. Quite candidly, they are fine if some people don't like them (we will introduce a concept of "shrinking your circle" later in the book).

I admire people who stand firmly on whatever principles they have, even if I don't always agree with them. You know where they stand. I also have found it to be true that when you try to please everybody, you end up pleasing no one, which is why we need to stop comparing ourselves to others. You need to be you at all times.

The greats also have the discipline to work on the things they necessarily didn't want to do but knew they had to in order to be great. Mike Tyson, one of the all-time great heavyweight boxers, had a trainer named Cus D'Amato, who once said, "Discipline is doing what you hate to do, but do it like you love it."[7] Wow. Just wow. Quotes like this one will motivate you on the days you are "not in the mood" to do the work!

What I've found is that the true greats in all walks of life consistently pursue excellence. They do so with incredible focus and discipline. Yes, they had a certain amount of talent, drive, work ethic, a plan, and a support system. But their setbacks were mere speed bumps in the road that forced them to take one or two steps back but then leap dozens of steps ahead of their peers. Just ask any of these people about their "failures," and they likely can't articulate an actual failure but would tell you a story about a loss or setback they eventually overcame.

One example of this for me was when I left a former employer through what's called a "mutual separation." The action was initiated by management (my boss) and accepted by the employee (me). I was going through a tough time outside the workplace, and while I was still doing a decent job, I was oftentimes distracted, couldn't focus throughout the entire day, and wasn't really the best version of myself. At the time I vehemently disagreed with my boss on this, and I blamed external factors and made excuses. But after reflecting I can now see I was the one to blame, not my boss. I've since learned and now coach my clients that we are the ones responsible for the outcomes in our life, both good and bad.

Thankfully, the game of life is generally a long one, and we can recover from setbacks like my example. Simon Sinek references another relevant concept in another one of his books called the *Infinite Game.*

"The world is consumed by finite thinking. There's a decline of trust and innovation when we think in a linear way. Winning in finite games is a temporary state. What we should be focused on is the long game." Sinek argues that, as an example, business has the following characteristics of an infinite game:

- Known and unknown players.
- New players can join at any time.
- Each player has their own strategy.
- There is no set of fixed rules.
- There is no beginning or end.[8]

But what most people or businesses do is play the finite game with linear thinking. One of the core messages of *Make the Adjustment* is to help you play the long game, the *Infinite Game* if you will, and also help you manage the hourly, daily, weekly, and monthly challenges you will most likely face, because life is hard and oftentimes unpredictable.

Which leads us to another reason people don't accomplish their goals: They are too busy comparing their own lives to others on social media. Get off of it for a while. Trust me, it will be worth it.

In a study by the National Institutes of Health, they found a direct correlation between social media use of 3.5 hours per day to mental health issues, mainly anxiety and depression. The prominent risk factors for anxiety and depression emerging from this study comprised time spent, activity, and the addiction to social media.

When people like or comment on their uploaded photos and videos, some people experience anxiety from social media related to fear of loss, which causes them to respond quickly and check all their friends' messages on a regular basis. These studies also noted that individuals who are involved in online video games, texting, using apps on mobile phones, and so on are more likely to experience anxiety and depression.[9]

Interestingly, passive activity in social media use such as reading posts is more strongly associated with depression than doing active use like making posts and creating content.[10] So if you are going to log in to social media accounts, spend more time focusing on creating content than consuming content. If you are going to consume content, only "follow" positive media channels that bring positive energy and inspire you as opposed to doom and gloom or something that causes you to be sad or jealous. The time is now to start creating the life you want to lead and achieving the goals you want to achieve.

In this chapter, we've identified the competencies and characteristics of what helps the greats be successful, and we've provided examples of some of the most successful humans on the planet. This chapter also helps you identify your purpose and a clear understanding of your "why" to start exploring what adjustments you will want to make.

Once you are clear on who you want to be and what you want to achieve, the next chapter will delve into a deeper understanding of self-awareness. Being truly self-aware is a critical component in your journey of knowing your strengths and weaknesses and how you will be able to better manage yourself when obstacles most certainly present themselves.

ADJUSTMENTS TO MAKE

1. Your "why" must be crystal clear.
2. Understanding your greater purpose provides you with the discipline needed on days you are not in a good mood or don't feel well.
3. Whatever gets you excited each day is your intrinsic motivation. Follow that feeling and trust it.
4. Reflect and be honest with yourself as to why you haven't yet attained some of your goals.
5. Become comfortable with who you really are and be less worried about what other people think.
6. Have a long-term view of your goals and play the infinite game, always.
7. Create more social media content than you consume, and only follow positive social media channels.

CHAPTER 2

Emotional Intelligence (EQ): Self Awareness

Did you know that only 33 percent of people are truly self-aware?[1] Think about that for a second. Almost all of us think we are self-aware, but statistically, two-thirds of us are not. I used to think I was a relatively self-aware person, only to find out in my mid-thirties that who I *thought* I was, wasn't aligned to who other people thought I was!

If you are not familiar with the term "emotional intelligence," it was first coined by Michael Beldoch in 1964[2] but popularized by researchers Peter Salovey and John Mayer in 1990. Psychologist Daniel Goleman, of whom I am a huge fan, later popularized it in 1995.[3]

The definition of emotional intelligence (otherwise known as emotional quotient, or EQ) is the ability to understand, use, and manage your own emotions in positive ways to relieve stress, communicate more effectively, empathize with others, overcome challenges, and defuse conflict. EQ is quite different from IQ (intelligence quotient), as IQ is a measure of a person's cognitive abilities, including reasoning, problem solving, memory, and other mental capabilities.

Some believe that we as humans are born with a certain level of IQ, fully developed and unable to increase. But this in fact is not the case and one's IQ has the capability of increasing or decreasing throughout one's lifetime.[4] Similarly, EQ is also something we can improve upon throughout our entire lives.

Intelligence Quotient (IQ)	Classification	Percentile
>130	Very Superior	>98%
120-129	Superior	91-97%
110-119	High Average	75-90%
90-109	Average	25-73%
90-89	Low Average	9-23%
70-79	Borderline	2-8%
<70	Very Low	<2%

IQ Ranges

Emotional Intelligence (EQ)	Definition
Self Regard	How I feel about myself
Self Awareness	What I see in me
Self Control	What I say and what I do
Social Perception	What others percieve about me
Social Effectiveness	My ability to get things done through others

EQ Overview

The first level of EQ is self-awareness, which is defined as having the ability to understand our own personality, actions, values, beliefs, emotions, and thoughts in the moment they happen. We will address three additional levels of EQ beyond self-awareness throughout this book, as well as illustrated above.

My personal journey of understanding EQ started in 2005 when my employer decided to run 360 reviews for all leaders. A 360 is a type of performance review where multiple people contribute anonymous feedback in order for the reviewed leader to gain valuable insights on how they can improve. The leader completes a self-assessment and invites their boss, all of their direct reports, three peers, and three business partners outside of their division but with whom they interact regularly to provide constructive feedback.

At this point in time, I was thirty-five years old and had been a relatively successful sales executive and manager. From a self-awareness perspective, I thought other people would say I was hard working, a skillful communicator, enthusiastic, a good problem solver, confident, and resilient. I also thought they might say I struggled with detail orientation, conflict management, or decisiveness.

After the review was complete, my manager scheduled a meeting to provide me with feedback. And with most 360 reviews, there's a lot of positive feedback and some constructive. But after their first 360 review most people go straight to the negative feedback and focuses on the areas of development more than the positive feedback.

The thing from my first 360 that jumped out most to me was, "Chris is not a good listener." I was stunned because I hear everything people say and can repeat it back to them! I couldn't believe it and took this feedback too personally at the time. The company then assigned all leaders an executive coach who helped work with them on the areas needing improvement. The coach I worked with for nine months helped with my active listening skills, and my second round of 360 performance review scores improved slightly in this area but still weren't where I hoped they would be.

Then in 2017, at a different company, we did 360 reviews for the entire leadership team. Again, I willingly participated and was genuinely curious to see if my new colleagues would provide me with any new insights where I could improve, and I thought for sure listening wouldn't be an issue. Again, I was wrong. "Chris struggles to stay engaged in meetings;

oftentimes seems distracted and doesn't listen well." *Huh? What?* Again, I was shocked by this feedback and truly couldn't believe it.

My manager then thought it would be a good idea for us to participate in an emotional intelligence training class, which also included a personalized EQ assessment from a company called BlueEQ. This excited me because I had read some books on emotional intelligence, and we would be diving much deeper into this topic. This assessment would provide feedback in the five primary areas of EQ, which included:

- Self-regard
- Self-awareness
- Self-control
- Social perception
- Social effectiveness

Low and behold on my BlueEQ assessment, the feedback was relatively strong in the areas of self-regard, self-awareness, self-control, and social effectiveness, but the biggest area of development was social perception—mainly mindfulness, which is defined as "the ability to be fully present and aware of one's thoughts, feelings, and surroundings in the moment they are happening."

Ah-ha! That's it! That was the feedback that resonated with me. It wasn't that I wasn't listening to people, it was that people perceived me to not be present and in the moment; that my mind would drift if I lost interest in a conversation or meeting.

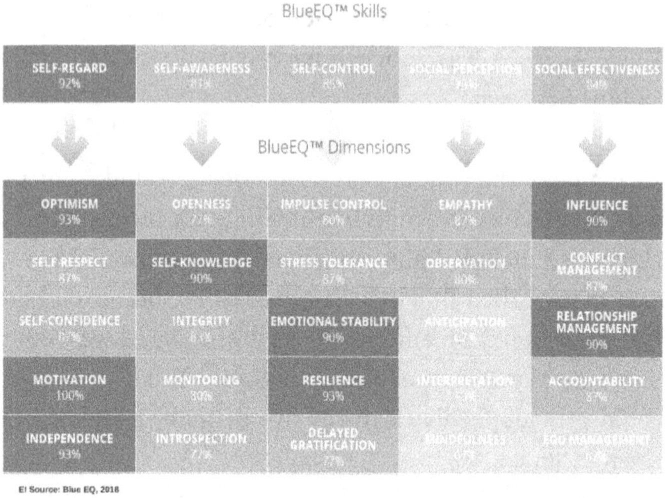

BlueEQ™ Skills

SELF-REGARD	SELF-AWARENESS	SELF-CONTROL	SOCIAL PERCEPTION	SOCIAL EFFECTIVENESS
92%	[illegible]	[illegible]	[illegible]	[illegible]

BlueEQ™ Dimensions

OPTIMISM	OPENNESS	IMPULSE CONTROL	EMPATHY	INFLUENCE
93%	[illegible]	80%	[illegible]	90%
SELF-RESPECT	SELF-KNOWLEDGE	STRESS TOLERANCE	OBSERVATION	CONFLICT MANAGEMENT
87%	90%	87%	[illegible]	87%
SELF-CONFIDENCE	INTEGRITY	EMOTIONAL STABILITY	ANTICIPATION	RELATIONSHIP MANAGEMENT
[illegible]	[illegible]	90%	[illegible]	90%
MOTIVATION	MONITORING	RESILIENCE	INTERPRETATION	ACCOUNTABILITY
100%	80%	93%	[illegible]	87%
INDEPENDENCE	INTROSPECTION	DELAYED GRATIFICATION	MINDFULNESS	EGO MANAGEMENT
93%	[illegible]	[illegible]	[illegible]	[illegible]

EI Source: Blue EQ, 2018

BlueEQ Assessment

That level of feedback had an immediate and marked impact on my development. Never again would I multitask in a meeting, never again would I multitask during a one-on-one conversation. I turned off my email or any other distractions when I was working on the core activities of my job. I started to "single task" and really focused on staying present in the conversation, meeting, or task at hand. Trust me, it's something I still work on but have made marked improvements through the years.

It's funny, many leaders I coach fear 360 reviews. They're afraid to be vulnerable, as if being vulnerable is a sign of weakness. I completely disagree. It takes courage and a mindset of continuous improvement in order to be the best possible leader and person you can be. Retired Navy Seal and now motivational speaker David Goggins once said,

"Every day, you are either getting better or getting worse. The choice is yours."[5]

One reason I am writing this book is to help people live in reality and no longer have their heads in the sand or have a false sense of who they really are. I want to help people understand the gaps between who they think they are (self-awareness) versus how others perceive them (social perception).

As I spend more time in my leadership coaching business, I find the math that at least two-thirds of the people can improve in the area of emotional intelligence to be accurate. We all can improve our EQ, but it requires a focus and willingness to want to improve, no matter the field or position. Whether it's C-suite leaders, salespeople, engineers, programmers, accountants, construction workers, and so on.

Emotional intelligence includes having the ability to understand and manage our emotions, as well as recognize and influence the emotions of those around us. Daniel Goleman, who originally coined the term, also found "for star performers in all jobs, in every field, emotional competence (EQ) is twice as important as purely cognitive abilities (IQ). For success at the highest levels, including leadership positions, emotional competence accounts for virtually the entire advantage."[6]

At one of my former employers, I was responsible for a global study around the science and statistics behind what drove the top performers to be great in the roles we were assessing. We tested people in management, sales, recruiting, finance, back-office support, and others. We used the Wonderlic Assessment test as the primary instrument to measure these factors. The Wonderlic test measures the cognitive ability and problem-solving aptitude of prospective employees who must answer fifty multiple choice questions in twelve minutes. The test is designed to create an atmosphere of quick thinking and a mild amount of stress, and only an approximated 5 percent of test subjects complete it in the given time.

After baselining more than 1,200 employees on the Wonderlic, we discovered that motivation, drive, and optimism (high EQ) proved to be the key indicators of someone's success, not solely their cognitive ability. These three important keys to success have nothing to do with IQ or how "smart" we are.

REFLECTION POINT

Ask yourself: Are you motivated? Are you driven? How optimistic are you? Do you believe you can make the changes necessary to succeed? Because I've found that making the adjustment is difficult for people due to one of three things:

1. They lack self-awareness and don't know they need to make the adjustment.
2. They know they need to make a change, but lack the motivation, drive, discipline, strategy to plan, or knowledge of where to begin.
3. They know what to do but lack the will, drive, or motivation, or they are afraid to make changes because of the discomfort it will cause.

Reflect on those three possible answers, and be honest with yourself. Are you ready to make the adjustment?

Rubber starts to hit the road here. Because reflecting like this can be tough when you start to realize you are the one responsible for not attaining your goals. It's not other people or the external factors. It's you.

Let's live in a world of what currently is, not what might be. Find the figurative mirror and take a look. What do you see? How do you look? Say something… What's your voice inflection? What's your body language like? How do you present yourself to the world? What words would other people use to describe you? All of this adds up to what's called your "personal brand."

Once you have a clear understanding of who you think you are, I want you to take some time to ask your five to ten closest friends or family members the words they would use to describe you. Only ask people you truly trust because they need to be honest with you. *Crucial Conversations* is a terrific book about feedback and says we need to be *candid* and *kind* when giving important feedback to others. So let these people know you are on a journey of personal or professional growth when you ask for this feedback.

Accurately assessing your self-awareness is the core of everything. It describes your ability to not only understand your strengths and weaknesses but to recognize your emotions and their effect on you (or your team's) performance.

According to research by organizational psychologist Tasha Eurich, working with colleagues who aren't self-aware can cut a team's success in half and lead to increased stress and decreased motivation.[7]

If you understand your own emotions and their impact on your performance, you know what you are feeling and why—and how it helps or hurts what you are trying to do. You sense how others see you, and your self-image reflects that larger reality. You have an accurate sense of your strengths and limitations, which gives you a realistic self-confidence. It also gives you clarity on your values and sense of purpose so you can be more decisive when you set a course of action.

According to the book *Daily Stoic*, we need to look through the lens of humility when it comes to our level of self-awareness. Authors Ryan Holiday and Stephen Hanselman reference that we need to look through the lens of humility.[8] We need to have a truly open mind. Even if it's painful to look at, we need to push through that pain. It's important to take stock of everything, even if it's uncomfortable. The stoics say there's only one thing we as humans truly control, and that is our mind.

The stoics will also tell you that people can improve their intelligence under two variables. One is remaining humble; the other is identifying the flaws in our thinking and biases.

Because the stoics remind us to have an open mind, this is what I will be asking of you as I guide you through all the theories and concepts throughout this book.

You also may start to realize early on in this book that I connect many popular and well-researched theories and concepts that I've applied to my life or coached others to apply to their lives that have worked.

Another example of this was when I took an assessment called StrengthsFinder. One of my identified strengths was ideation, which is defined when someone is "delighted when [they] discover, beneath the complex surface, an elegantly simple concept to explain why things are the way they are."[9] An idea is a connection. My brain is always looking for these connections and is intrigued when an obscure connection can link seemingly disparate phenomena.

Others have said I am creative, original, conceptual, or even smart. Perhaps. But what I know for certain is that connecting ideas and then executing against promising ideas is thrilling, and we will be doing a lot of it in this book. Again, this book is about growth, and growth comes from a place of discomfort.

In chapter 3, we will continue to get uncomfortable, because I am going to ask you to do something that might feel unnatural: Shrink your inner circle.

ADJUSTMENTS TO MAKE
1. The vast majority of people in this world are truly not self-aware.
2. Someone who is emotionally intelligent has elevated levels of:

- Self-regard, which includes: optimism, self-respect, motivation, self-confidence, and independence
- Self-awareness, which includes: openness, self-knowledge, introspection, monitoring, and integrity
- Self-control, which includes: impulse control, stress tolerance, emotional stability, resilience, and delayed gratification
- Social perception, which includes: empathy, observation, anticipation, interpretation, and mindfulness
- Social effectiveness, which includes: influence, conflict management, relationship management, accountability, and ego management

3. We need to identify our areas of strengths and weaknesses. "What am I good at?" "Where do I want to get better?" Review the list above and try to first identify your areas of strength. Then choose one category plus one to two of the subcategories listed within as areas of development you would like to improve upon.

4. Compare your list with five to ten of your closest friends and family to see what they believe your strengths and weaknesses are.

5. Compare your list to their list to gain alignment on your future areas of development and improvement.

6. Pick one or two, but no more than three, areas where you would like to improve.

CHAPTER 3

Shrink Your Inner Circle

I've found there are two types of people in this world. Those who bring you energy or those who take your energy. Choose to spend your time with those who provide you with positive energy and not those who take life out of you.

I don't know about you, but I currently have over one thousand "friends" on Facebook. But do I really know more than one thousand people? I suppose I've met them or know them through mutual friends, but do I really know all of them? Likely not. I mean, how many of those people really know what's really going on in my life? Very few, likely less than a dozen or so.

When I was young my father once said, "Chris, you'd be lucky that at the end of your life to have five genuinely great friends, those who were with you through thick and thin. No matter what happens to you, no matter what you do, they will be there and have your back." I didn't fully understand the meaning of what he was saying in my youth. But as I got older, I began to see his point, especially in 2020, when I endured a life experience that statistically about half of adults live through: a divorce.

Divorce is a terrible thing, not only for the two people going through it but more so for the kids. I was married to my now ex-wife for twenty-four years, and we had three children together. I won't go much into it, but I will say we went to counseling and tried to sort out our issues. In the end we were unable to. I can say with some level of pride that we agreed to work through a mediator, and that process helped us get to an outcome that was about as amicable as could be. Even though I will always carry guilt and sadness over it, I am proud of how my ex-wife and I handled that adversity and are still civil and kind to each other.

Telling our kids was without a doubt the worst day of my life. As you would expect, it was rough. What I found even more fascinating was, once the news was out with our friends and family, only a few people were really there to support me.

I spent many years supporting others as a leader in the workplace and thought I'd been a supportive friend. But when I was the one at a low point, I was stunned how few people were not there for me when I needed them most. The most common thing people would say is, "Whatever you need, let me know." And for fifty years of my life, I never asked anyone for anything. But when I was in a position where I needed that support, even the people who said "whatever you need" didn't come through when asked.

Thankfully, a handful of people were there for me. I am so incredibly grateful to them, and they know who they are.

They would call or stop by unannounced to check in on me; take me out for coffee, lunch, drinks, or dinner to just talk; and make sure I was doing okay. I get emotional thinking about these people, because they helped me reframe my self-worth and know I was a good person and father and that everything would be okay.

I didn't set out to shrink my circle after my divorce. However, those fewer but much closer relationships outweighed the value of having my supposed one thousand "friends" on social media.

I started to spend more time on myself and with my kids, parents, and closest friends. And each day, my self-esteem and physical and emotional well-being improved. I actually started to find even better professional career opportunities, and just like the exercise in chapter 1, I reframed who I was, what was most important to me, and where I would spend my time.

One of the people I've always enjoyed spending time with was one of my mentors and first manager in business, Bob Dickey. He's always had a pretty tight circle of friends, and when I told him about this book, we had an interesting conversation. I shared how much I respected the people who stood out on their own, were unique, had an opinion on things, and weren't wishy-washy. They didn't really care what other people thought of them. They were always true to themselves and weren't seeking to please others. Without a doubt, Bob fits this mold.

We then started joking about this, because for many years of my life I was always trying to please people. In hindsight, while I was busy trying to please others, I wasn't really pleasing myself and wasn't content with my life.

In the *Daily Stoic*, the first two core tenets of the stoics are self-examination and the company you keep.[1] In the previous chapter, we dug into self-examination via EQ and self-awareness, so now let's move onto reviewing the company you currently keep. More importantly, this chapter will encourage you to think about the company you would *like* to keep.

Motivational speaker and entrepreneur Jim Rohn once said that "we are the average of the five people we spend the most time with,"[2] and I believe this to be true. I have been extremely fortunate in my life to have spent time with hundreds of successful athletes and leaders, and I tried to learn what made them great and apply those lessons in my own life as a person and as a leader.

So, when going through adversity, I had to make some difficult decisions around some of my personal and professional relationships. If the people I was spending my time with were truly on my side, supporting me, and adding value to my life, then I needed to find time for them. However, if the people I was with were giving me anxiety or causing me pain or sadness, then I needed to create some separation and distance from them.

I often give some great advice to working mothers with whom I've managed in the past or currently coach in the present. When they get stressed out or are feeling like they aren't doing enough at work or for their family, I simply say,

"It's difficult to take care of others if you don't first take care of yourself." So, we must do whatever we need at all costs to protect our own inner peace and happiness.

When I first did this exercise in my mid-twenties, I had to break away from some relationships both in and out of the workplace, because I knew in the long run those people were not going to be good for me, nor would they help me attain the goals I wanted in life. In fact, some of these connections were holding me back or, even worse, taking me down a dark path that I know would have led to me troubling times and far from my goals.

With that, when it comes to shrinking your circle, in 2018 author Scott Gerber wrote a *Harvard Business Review* article which stated, "Carefully curate your most trusted, inner circle and you'll be surprised at how much more valuable you'll become to the larger community of people who care about the same things you do."[3] I couldn't agree with this more, so let's review the process in which we can start shrinking our circle.

The first step is what we did in chapter 2, becoming self-aware. We have to ask ourselves, are you in control of the relationships in your life, or are you giving up control to others? Does each relationship in your life add or decrease value? Do these relationships help you achieve your goals, or do they deter you from your goals?

Scott Gerber also said, "If you are not deciding the rules of engagement and making deliberate choices about who you are spending time with, then you need to take back that control. Start by making a plan to lessen your time investment in people and activities that make unrewarding demands on you until you can fully withdraw from the person, commitment, or activity."[4] Setting boundaries becomes paramount in your equation for making the adjustments necessary to attain your goals.

Reflect back on chapter 1 when I asked you to assess how you are spending your time and what activities are you doing. Where did you spend your time in the past week? The thought process here is to ask, "Were those activities worth your time or not worth your time? What would you do again or invest more time in? What would you cut entirely?" Ask yourself if how you're spending your time is aligned with your most deeply held values. If it's not, then drop it, even if that has the potential to put you in an uncomfortable position with friends or colleagues.

The last step is to assess who you are spending your time with. Tim Dahi, an author, and attorney, once said, "The prime candidates (you want to spend your time with) are those loyal friends whose level of commitment to you is not diminished by time or distance. Friends who will enable your growth and are not threatened by your success."[5]

That's the question: Who is on *your* team? When you win, is that person happy for you, or are they jealous? Or even worse, are they resentful? Remember, relationships should not be transactional. Our loyal friends are there to really help, not because there is the expectation of reciprocity but because by supporting you, being useful, and being generous builds social capital and makes those friendships genuine.

As you shrink your inner circle, you'll begin thinking of yourself as the CEO of your life. As you forge deeper, more authentic relationships with smaller numbers of people who are genuinely important to you, you will gain more context into their wants and needs, and they will likewise develop a fuller understanding of you. Which leads us into chapter 4, something I like to call having an "owner's mentality."

ADJUSTMENTS TO MAKE

- Be selective about the company you would like to keep.
  - Select people who you want to be on your "team" and want you to win.
- Be authentic and true to yourself.
- Don't be a people pleaser.
- You can't take care of others until you first take care of yourself.
- Take control and choose relationships with those who will support you, no matter what.
- Make a list of who you currently spend your time with.
  - Do these people bring you energy or drain your energy?
  - Choose the friends who will enable your growth and are not threatened by your success.
  - Does spending time with this person add value to your life or decrease value?
  - Do you really trust this person? With your family, children? What do they say when you are not in the room? Do they have your back?
  - Choose people you want to build and maintain a long-term friendship and relationship with.
  - Allocate time each week or month for these people, ideally in person, whenever possible.

CHAPTER 4

Owner's Mentality

"An owner can't quit."

—JOHN STUART, FOUNDER AND CEO OF

ZEEK TEK AND ZEEK DIGITAL

Back in 1996, I started working for a small IT staffing company called New Boston Systems, and this company was in hyper growth mode. The external factors in the market were favorable, and the management team was hiring hungry, driven, strong character people. I was lucky to join when I did. I started in an outside sales role, which was all new to me as I hadn't been in professional sales and business development previously. But after a tough first year I started to figure things out, and many people on our team were performing very well compared to other divisions outside the greater Boston area.

Our team was exceeding goals, and as a result one of the more successful recruiters, John Stuart, earned a management promotion. He relocated his family to expand our presence in the southeastern part of the US and grow his career. At the time, I didn't realize how lucky we all were to be working with such great people, in a great industry, in one of the best companies in our sector. If you worked hard, were coachable, and could handle adversity, the sky was the limit. John was about three years ahead of me professionally. He ended up becoming a great mentor and friend, and he is now a client of MTA Consultancy.

In 1999 our company continued to expand, and my manager, Bob Dickey, asked if I wanted to stay in the suburbs of Boston or if I would be willing to relocate to Connecticut and open a new office, which is what I ultimately decided to do. Upon accepting this role, I asked all leaders in my company what their best "silver bullet" advice was. So, when I called John, the first thing he referenced was what he called having an "owner's mentality."

My recollection of that conversation was, "Chris, even though the company is paying for all of this, you need to act like this is your own money. Act like you are paying for everything in the business as if it were coming out of your own personal checking account with every decision you make. Hiring people, the corporate lease agreement, client entertainment, business travel—everything. Do not spend the company's money unless you would spend it with your own money."

As a new leader, this was fantastic advice and is something I've always carried with me. When writing this book, I couldn't help but reach back out to John to gain further insights on what owner's mentality means to him now. In 2016, both John and I left our company of twenty-plus years, and he went on to become a true "owner" when he founded

Zeek Tek, a technology staffing and solutions company based in Northern California. He's already gone on to expand his business through a subsidiary called Zeek Digital, which offers on-demand marketers for staffing companies.

John said, "You know, Chris, not much has changed, as I feel like I've always acted like an owner. And when you are an owner, you have to be all in. You have to have the mentality where there's no other option for you. This isn't just a job, it's your company. And your employees and your family are fully reliant on you to guide and support them to attain their personal and professional goals."

When John said this, I couldn't help but agree, because I too became an "owner" of my own firm, MTA Consultancy LLC, in 2023 with a core focus on executive coaching, leadership and sales training, advisory services, and keynote speaking. When I started my company, I was researching entrepreneurship deeply and consuming as much content as I could. One book in particular really resonated with me, *Burn the Boats* by Matt Higgins.

The key concept from *Burn the Boats* is that there's a bold and highly effective tactic seen throughout history—when you want to motivate yourself or your troops for success, you destroy all opportunities for retreat and fully commit to the mission. They burn their boats. It's win or perish, and the clarity of having no other options and desperation propels them to victory.[1]

I had executive recruiters calling me and pitching jobs in the corporate world. But I never again wanted someone else to dictate my decisions, income expectations, what I did or didn't do, or my future. The safe play for me was to take plan B with a steady job and earn a predictable income… but deep down, I wouldn't have been happy. I committed and burned the boats!

I'd also love to tell you I'm independently wealthy and that money didn't matter. But it does. As I am writing this book, I've invested more than $50,000 into starting up my new business and ran up a fair amount of additional debt. But since the day I opened MTA Consultancy, I've had zero anxiety about my career. I am in the right seat doing the work I love to do, helping people attain better outcomes by solving often complex problems they haven't been able to solve for years.

When you start your own company, or any endeavor that you deeply care about, I genuinely believe you have to burn the boats and not have a plan B. There is only plan A. Interestingly, the extraordinarily successful musician Ed Sheeran once said on the Howard Stern show, "Don't have a plan B. Because if you have a plan B, when things get difficult you will quit. If you only have plan A, you will succeed, because you'll just be like, I have to do it, so it's going to happen."[2]

I totally can relate to this in a few separate ways. When people asked me at ten years old what I wanted to do when I grew up, my answer was "to be a professional baseball player." And that answer *never* changed for me. People would tell me I was delusional, but I paid them no mind. I was on my path. I had my plan A. I loved playing baseball and felt in my heart I could make it. I worked harder than anyone I knew at my craft. I had belief in myself when very few other people did, other than my parents and best friends, of course, who believed I could achieve my goal.

Similar to Ed's quote that resonates with me is when my former Coach Coffie once said, "Chris, is this something you want, or do you have to have it?" Everyone wants it, whatever it is: money, fame, career, physical fitness… But if you have to have it, you will find a way to figure it out.

So, without a plan B, you execute on plan A with strategy, passion, and purpose. It must consume you, but in a healthy way. Everything you do for your plan A is because you love to do it and it's your destiny. Deep down, only you know who you are and what you want. Nobody else can live your life other than you, and you must do what makes you happy.

Ed Sheeran went on to say he got paid £200 (approximately $250 USD) at one of his first paying gigs. He said he knew everything would be all right because he could make a few hundred pounds every time he played and his life would be okay.[3] Of course, after thousands of hours of mastering the guitar, vocals, and his unique style when performing, he went on to become one of the most popular recording artists to ever come out of the UK. I believe whether his net worth was $20,000 or $20,000,000, he would be happy because he was the one who chose his plan A.

Similarly, for me, when starting my business, my first year's revenue and income (if annualized) was less than half what I earned the year before. But I was happier. My work has a greater purpose. I understood my "why" not only in my business but in my personal life as well. And as I write this, my revenue and run rate for year two (2024) is about to match what I previously earned in 2022 as an employee working for someone else.

Therein is the formula for being a happy "owner." We all need something to do, someone to love, and something to look forward to. With "something to do," you need to be passionate about what you do. With "someone to love," everyone needs a person who will love them no matter what and makes them a better version of themselves. And with "something to look forward to," you can manifest your future once you decide to draw a line in the sand and live your life with passion, purpose, and persistence so that nothing can derail you.

So, if you are going to spend the next ten, twenty, thirty, or forty-plus years earning a living, it's worth finding something you genuinely love to do. And do it with someone you love while planning your future together.

Someone with an owner's mentality is a person who owns their behavior, owns their actions, owns their outcomes, and owns their mistakes. They alone are responsible for themselves. And once you can manage yourself, it becomes infinitely easier to manage other people and hold them to the same standards. Someone with an owner's mentality takes ownership of everything that happens to them (and their people or team), both good and bad.

The final reason having an owner's mentality is required is you will have to lead the changes you are implementing as well as understand why others around you may or may not accept these changes. The vast majority of people resist change, which will be discussed in further detail in the next chapter, "Understanding and Leading Change."

ADJUSTMENTS TO MAKE

1. You are the owner, and "the owner can't quit."
2. Someone with an owner's mentality:
   - Owns their behavior;
   - Owns their outcomes;
   - Owns their mistakes;
   - Spends money as if it was their own, even if they are spending their company's or someone else's money;
   - Focuses all of their energy on plan A and doesn't ever consider plan B as an option;
   - Is passionate;
   - Finds a life partner who challenges them (in a healthy way) to continuously improve; and
   - Manifests their future.

CHAPTER 5

Understanding and Leading Change

"The measure of intelligence is the ability to change."

—ALBERT EINSTEIN

If it hasn't become apparent yet, this book is primarily about navigating change, why some people can make the adjustments to incrementally improve, and why many people struggle to make them. It's fascinating when you ask someone the simple question, "Do you want to improve at ___________," the answer is almost always yes. But when you start walking someone through the process of what it's going to take to improve, they opt out, run out of energy and focus, or quit at some point along the way.

An example of this is a CEO with whom I worked. They are successful from a career and income perspective, running a multi-million-dollar company. A past colleague referred me to work with this company, and part of the program included implementing 360 reviews.

What's interesting about this story is this CEO approved the 360 reviews for all of their managers but not themselves, which I thought was strange. What were they afraid of? I said, "You're the boss (and paying the invoice), so you don't have to do this. But I would encourage you to participate as it shows your team that the C-suite leads by example."

Their answer was fascinating when they said, "Why would I want to subject myself to that? I've already been successful at leading this company. Besides, I really don't want to know what people have to say about me."

I was floored. This CEO is a successful person who had a look and demeanor that exuded confidence. But when you peel the onion back, they were incredibly insecure. And I get it, this behavior was actually quite normal, because deep down everyone has these negative thoughts in their head and doesn't always want to face them.

Based on those I've worked with, coached, and my own personal experience, there are a few main reasons why people resist change of any type, including behavior change:

- Fear
- Perceived risk
- Discomfort
- Past negative experience
- Self-imposed (we get in our own way, defeatist attitude, negative self-talk, and so on)
- Irrational thoughts (not thinking logically)

Those last two are important: "self-imposed" and "irrational thoughts." Why as humans do we get in our own way? What are we afraid of? What's the worst thing that can happen? Why do we do this to ourselves?

We use negative self-talk or have a defeatist attitude even before we start or give up far too soon when things get hard. A better question we need to reprogram our brains to say is, "What's the best thing that can happen if I make this change?" In my executive coaching business, I've begun to challenge my clients by stating, "Every time you say the word 'problem,' I want you to exchange that word for opportunity." It's fascinating how quickly their mindset shifts toward a solution and not overly focusing on the problem.

PROFESSIONAL LESSON

A concept called the "one by five theory" states for every one segment of time you spend defining the problem, spend five times longer working on the solution. As an example, in a thirty-minute meeting, you should be accurately framing the problem fives 5 minutes then spend the next twenty-five minutes actually solving it.

I, like you, have likely spent too much time in meetings just complaining about a problem which never gets solved.

Think about professional golf where there's the player and their caddy. For people who don't know the game, some people would argue the caddy is just the person out there carrying the player's clubs around and not doing much else. But the caddy's job is much bigger than that. They're also a coach and psychologist on the course with that player for their entire round. If you go to an event or if the mic is hot while watching TV, take a listen to the conversations. The player will say things like, "I stink today. Why do I even bother playing this game?" while the caddy is saying, "You're hitting it great, you're just getting some bad bounces. Let's just focus our energy on the next shot. Stay in the present and execute."

Let's dissect that conversation. The player is thinking about the past and everything that is going wrong (negative self-talk), and the caddy is thinking about the present (what can we control now). These at the core are the first two components of emotional intelligence, self-awareness, and self-control. Are you truly aware of how you are feeling in the moment, and do you have the ability to control those emotions?

When it comes to making excuses, I have a relevant personal story including negative self-talk as to why I didn't start a project. I was fortunate enough to bump into the one and only Jon Gordon once while attending a conference in Jacksonville Beach, Florida. Jon is a well-known motivational speaker and remarkably successful author, and I recognized him when he was walking across the lobby of the hotel. Sometimes you meet your heroes and they let you down. Jon didn't disappoint, and he was everything I thought he would be. His energy was infectious, and as I approached him, he was incredibly positive and upbeat. We had a great chat. When I told him I was thinking about writing a book someday, he said, "Just write it. What are you waiting for?" He then handed me a copy of one of his bestselling books, we shook hands, and after he walked away, I thought, *He's right. What am I waiting for?*

Only three months later I was introduced to Casey Jacox, a peer of mine in professional coaching who started his own business like I had not too long ago. Casey had also written a book and had a similar conversation I had with Jon. Casey said the same thing, "What are you waiting for? Just start writing…"

Those two conversations and words of encouragement got me started on this journey only three months afterward. Sometimes we just need a mentor, coach, or supportive person in our lives to get us on the right path.

REFLECTION POINT

We have to recognize when we come to an inflection point in our lives. These moments are critical in how we define the next number of years when it comes to our happiness, contentment, income, and mental health. It's decision time. Do I take action or not? Do I welcome change or resist?

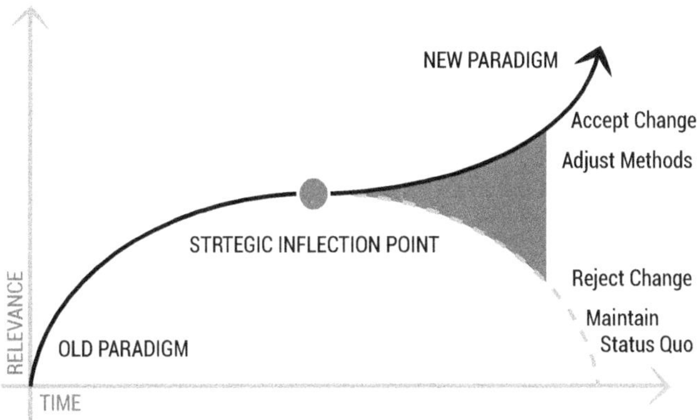

Reflection Point

It takes courage, but also a deeper understanding and self-awareness of why people resist change.

One of the issues with change is that we get comfortable—comfortable with our routine, our process, our day-to-day lives. It would take a lot of work to change, so why even bother? Everything is fine. Ugh! That word, "fine." I've always joked whenever someone says, "Everything is fine." Really listen to their tone and watch their body language. They're really not "fine," they are just comfortable with their situation. Again, remember the phrase, "Growth only comes from a place of discomfort."

One of my former colleagues and mentors, Dr. Rick Maybury, is an expert on professional development and adult learning. He is the president of the Knowles Johnson Institute of Graduate Studies, which offers a comprehensive integrated Master of Arts and Doctor of Philosophy programs in human and organizational development.

When I worked with him previously, he had some great advice on how to deal with change.[1] I interviewed him for this book, and he said, "We need to remember that change is experienced on the motive [or feeling] side of the brain, not the logical side of the brain."

Pause there on point number one. People are more likely to change when we feel a certain way. Most people don't actually change based on facts or data. People make decisions in life based on how they feel. And feelings can be fleeting, which is the reason we've discussed the aforementioned concepts of having a clear purpose, understanding your EQ, shrinking your circle, and having an owner's mentality.

Dr. Maybury went on to say, "There's also a difference between self-sustained change and externally driven change."

And there's point number two. Understanding the difference between externally imposed change versus self-sustained change. When it's externally imposed, we do what's necessary in the short term, and as soon as the pressure is off, we fall back to our old behaviors. But long term, self-imposed change occurs when we've come to the conclusion on our own, that we want this change. As a result, self-imposed change has a much greater chance of long-term success than short term, externally imposed change.

PROFESSIONAL DEVELOPMENT

Dr. Maybury said, "How do we typically, in organizations, get people to change? We start by giving them all the data. Right?"

"As an example in the workplace, if you tell someone you will give them a bonus for a certain task or goal, that's what they work toward. And once they get the bonus, they go back to whatever it was they were doing before. That's an example of externally driven short-term change. But is that really change? No. Change is internally driven. It is a sustained difference in the way we view the world, the way we think, and the way we act. So, it wouldn't require an external stimulus."

One of Dr. Maybury's key points is: When leaders micromanage to a system, scalability and growth doesn't come from people who follow templates, procedures, or protocols. Scalability and growth come from people who understand what they are trying to do, really listen to their client, and figure out new ways to adapt and improvise. That means they need to change the way they think in order to influence others along the way.

Let's apply this to leadership. As an example, once a business is behind their annual budget goals, some leaders start micromanaging their people. But in reality, what we want is for our people to be independent thinkers and problem solve their issues in real time. We want them to have the ability to adapt and improvise. And we want people who don't micromanage when they're out there on the floor or in the field. The leader cannot sit with every employee and diagnose or troubleshoot each of their issues in real time. We need to train, coach, and mentor our people so they are prepared to handle each situation as it presents itself.

We need to develop our staff so they can identify the business opportunities, adapt, and improvise, and do what's right for the client. What that means is our people need education, not training per se. They need leadership, not management.

If we require a salesperson to make fifty outgoing calls a day, and they make fifty, and that's the algorithm your business says works, then that salesperson had a so-called good day. But did they really have a good day? If they make fifty calls and no one picks up, that doesn't sound like a good day to me. What if they make fifty calls, speak with four prospects, and nothing comes of those conversations? *Hmmmm.* We need to understand as leaders that people will do what the template tells them to do as long as there are rewards or consequences.

Ultimately, we should be thinking more about outcomes than the activities and work the algorithm backward if we are not attaining outcomes we hoped for.

Dr. Maybury also said, "The bottom line is if we look at the neural studies, what we see is the process of change requires remapping of the brain, and people interpret this as personal risk because it's on the emotive side, not the logical side. And so, as change agents, we first need to understand where people are coming from and their comfort areas, what they're good at, and how they perceive themselves. And then what are we trying to get them to do, and how is it different from what they used to do? What is our growth path? It's an educational experience, not a training experience, because education is all about self-awareness and self-discovery and personal growth."

REFLECTION POINT

From a personal development perspective, I challenge you to take a step back and look at yourself in the third person, as if someone else was watching you right now. What would a person say? What advice would they give? Doing this helps put fresh eyes on a problem or challenge.

Another way to do this is to start with a blank whiteboard, like you were coaching someone else. What advice would you give that person? Keep the focus on solving the root cause of the issue or challenge you are trying to improve.

After reflection, it's important for us to understand our comfort level or propensity to change, as there are four types of people when it relates to change:

1. Innovator
2. Early adopter
3. Fence sitter
4. Laggard

In what's called the diffusion of innovation theory in a study done by Boston University, researchers discovered through studies the innovators only comprise about 2.5 percent of people in this world.[2] They are the groundbreakers and trailblazers, and they usually have more ideas than time to execute. And they love change. Their motto is "let's break it and see what happens!"

Early adopters also have a high propensity to accept change. They don't always have the new idea, but they can connect the dots to see a promising idea and be the first to try it. It could be a new product they buy, or a new service they sell, but they get excited about the future and how it could be different and better long before the majority of the population sees it. This group comprises about 13.5 percent of the population.[3]

Next are the vast majority of people, about 68 percent of the population, who are fence sitters.[4] They remain neutral and undecided. They oftentimes will sit back, watch, and wait to see if the new product, idea, or service works. And they won't do much until they see it working. But once they do, they can get on board. The upside to a fence sitter is they don't struggle with the trials and tribulations of trouble shooting the challenges and issues that come with a change. They also might miss out on earlier opportunities if and when the change works.

And lastly is the laggard, the remaining 16 percent of the population.[5] Laggards absolutely resist any and all change until they finally accept, are forced, or never adapt change and eventually become irrelevant.

Let's close the chapter by taking a quick assessment to identify where you might fall when it comes to change.

A. Change for the sake of change is disruptive.
"I'm not a fan of change. I prefer things stay the same and predictable."

B. Change without purpose is not preferred.
"I am okay with change only if it is necessary and I have the skills to manage the change."

C. I like change that I can control.
"I like to create change, but I much prefer to be in control of change I can create."

D. My motto is, Let's break it and see what happens!
"I like change of almost any kind, whether it is imposed on me, or I create it. I do not have to be in control of the change."

Based on your response, person A is generally a laggard, person B is a fence sitter, person C is an early adopter, and person D is considered an innovator. What I do know about change is that if you answered D or C, or even B, you have an incredibly good chance to make a positive change both in and out of the workplace. For person A, if you really want to change, you will have to make some serious adjustments to your mindset and take on more of a growth versus fixed mindset, because A's typically resist change until it is absolutely necessary.

This exercise is intended to help you understand your level of self-awareness and how you respond to change, whether it's self-imposed or forced upon you. Because once we are self-aware, we then need to be in control of our words in actions, which will be discussed in the next chapter on the second level of emotional intelligence: mastering self-control.

ADJUSTMENTS TO MAKE
1. Be open minded and welcome change.
2. Understand the vast majority of people naturally resist change at first.
3. Remove the word "problem" and insert the word "opportunity."
4. The greatest obstacle of change is usually oneself.
5. Clearly define the problem you are trying to solve and spend five times longer on solving it.
6. Growth only comes from a place of discomfort. Get uncomfortable!
7. Accurately assess your current propensity to welcome change into your life or business.

Leveling Up Your Emotional Intelligence through Self-Control, Social Perception, and Social Effectiveness

In chapter 2, we discussed the first level of emotional intelligence is self-awareness, which we defined as having the ability to understand our own personality, actions, values, beliefs, emotions, and thoughts in the moment they are happening. "In the moment they are happening" is a key aspect of this.

How many times in your life did something happen that triggered you and made you unable to stay in control of your emotions *in the moment* it was happening? It's likely something you can recall because it happens to all of us. Emotional triggers generally happen due to a stimulus that causes someone to relive a traumatic event. Triggers can cause people to feel overwhelmed with sadness, anxiety, or panic. They can also cause flashbacks, which are vivid, often negative memories that may appear without warning.

I had an interesting conversation with a former colleague and current leader of a healthcare staffing firm recently. We are good friends, and he didn't want to be named in the book. But the story is truly relevant when it comes to the second level of EQ, which is self-control.

He said, "Chris, do you have any book recommendations on playing nice in the sandbox with other leaders, especially the leaders you don't see eye to eye with?"

I said, "How well read are you on emotional intelligence? Because what I've found is that you can't control another human being. All you can control is what you do and what you say to others."

He went on to say, "I tested off the charts for EQ when my manager had me take an assessment, and it was the highest he had seen. However, in the heat of the moment, I choose to argue and fight instead of collaborating. When I later reflect on the situation, I realize I was in the wrong and let my ego or pride get in the way in certain situations."

I can relate to him because this was me for a very long time. Candidly I think it's most humans, but I explained to him that EQ and self-control is something that can improve and become a superpower once we master it.

I went on to explain, "All information first goes through the brain via the amygdala and hits the limbic system first, which is the side of the brain that tells us how we feel. Then, after reflection, information eventually finds its way to the logical side of our brains, and we can see things for what they really are. The first level of emotional intelligence is self-awareness, so you have that, but the second level is self-control. So now that you know self-control is a flaw, you need to process information and situations in the moment and temper how you feel so the information can get to the logical side of your brain faster and, as a result, be more composed in the moment."

Continuing that thought, I said, "What I explain to people is after a heated conversation, within twenty-four hours we almost always calm down and see the conversation for what it was and what we would do differently next time. But the superpower of emotional intelligence is being able to do this within the actual moment of these conversations, not twenty-four hours later when it's too late."

PROFESSIONAL LESSON
In a white paper written by the Center for Creative Research, the study stated the primary causes of derailment in leaders involves deficits in emotional intelligence.[1] The three primary ones are:

- Difficulty in handling change;
- Not being able to work well within a team; and
- Poor relationships.

We discussed change in chapter 5, so let's take a deeper dive into not working well within a team or improving your poor relationships. I had a prior manager once ask what the common factor was in my poor relationships, meaning the people I struggled working with. The answer was me. I was the common factor in why it wasn't working. He also asked me what the common factor was in all the deals I didn't close in the past calendar year. Again, the answer was me. I was the common factor when things didn't go the way I wanted them to.

Simply stated, we can't (nor should we try to) control other people, but we can influence the way they think. It's a great mindset, especially for sales professionals, because if you closed 10 percent, 20 percent, or 30 percent of your deals this year but not 100 percent, that means someone else out there closed the client, but *you* didn't. Rather than blame your internal team, the competition, or other external factors, take accountability, review why you didn't win the business, and get better. Motivational speaker Brian Knight coined this tagline in his business, "Doesn't Matter, Get Better."[2] I love this mindset because it puts all the accountability on you and what you did or didn't do, causing us to have an internal locus of control.

READER EXERCISE

This chapter is primarily focused on controlling yourself: your own routine, habits, choices, and behaviors. So let's start with a simple exercise.

I want you to think of an interaction with another person who impacted you negatively. Think about the exact moment, time of day, where you were, and your surroundings. How did that person make you feel? Were you intimidated, bullied, scared, embarrassed? Try to put the emotions you felt in the moment into words. Write those feelings down. If you can think of another example of two, continue the exercise. Because once you are done, you've likely discovered the things that triggered you.

Getting triggered isn't as simple as overreacting. Emotional triggers are things that cause a strong, uncomfortable reaction to a stimulus that wouldn't normally cause that response. They can be memories, objects, or people. Better understanding your emotional triggers will make you truly self-aware. Once you know what bothers you and causes you to have strong emotions, you can train and rewire your brain to speed up the information that travels through your amygdala and limbic system to engage the logical side of your brain to make more rational decisions. People with a strong degree of self-control don't allow the feeling side of their brains to take over, which many times causes bad long-term decisions. Rather, these people can act in a calm demeanor and keep their emotions in check. Some people are born with this, but the good news for the rest of us when it comes to all things EQ, including self-control, we as humans can improve.

So now that you are in a logical state of mind, reading (or listening) to this book, you're likely calm, relaxed, and have a clear head. Using the logical side of your brain, you can reflect on these past negative experiences to see the situation for whatever it was. The key to self-control is this. Does it take you twenty-four to forty-eight hours to calm down after a heated exchange, or when you feel triggered or attacked? Or does it take you a few seconds to be self-aware and recognize how you feel, and then allow information to quickly flow through your limbic system (the way you feel) and get to the logical side of your brain so you can react with composure?

That's why self-control is a superpower. When the other side is losing their control, you are the one who remains calm, cool, and collected. I struggled with this for years as an extroverted, heart-on-my-sleeve type of person. But I had a couple of good managers who highlighted this as an area of growth for me, and I've improved. By no means am I perfect, but I now have a greater level of composure thanks to my increased self-awareness and self-control.

Here's another key piece of growth is understanding the difference between intent versus impact: As a lifelong optimist, I believe most human beings are good. *Inc. Magazine* supports this claim in an article in 2019 that stated that "83 percent of those surveyed believe that people are fundamentally good."[3] Sure there are bad people in the world (about 17 percent), but the vast majority of people are good. With that, let's discuss intentions for a minute.

How many times have you heard someone say, "I didn't intend to hurt their feelings when I said what I said. It's not my fault or problem they reacted that way." I used to say that too. But here's what I've learned about EQ and intentions. Eighty-three percent of people are well-intentioned, yet these same people hurt other people's feelings all the time. We've previously discussed that we as humans can't control other people, only influence them. So in the construct of understanding intent versus impact, an emotionally intelligent person wouldn't fall back on a weak statement like, "I didn't mean to hurt their feelings." Rather, an emotionally intelligent person would say, "I didn't intend to hurt their feelings, but I did. So because the impact of my words (or actions) had negative results, I need to make the adjustment and change what I say or do next time to get a better outcome from that interaction."

And this isn't to say you were necessarily in the wrong, but you can only control yourself, not other people. Perhaps when the other person is calm, it would be mature of you to say, "I didn't intend to impact you so negatively, so I want to apologize. How can we make this right? And what could I say or do differently next time?" This leads us to a key lesson upcoming in chapter 7 on locus of control. We cannot control what other people say or do, only what we say or do.

But back to my college baseball coach for a second. In 1991, Coach Boyd Coffie moved onto the professional ranks as a coordinator for player development for the former Cleveland Indians, now Cleveland Guardians, and later with the Colorado Rockies. Our whole team was all happy for Boyd and his new opportunity to transition from the college to professional ranks. But as a result of his departure, my senior year wasn't as much fun as it should have been. In Boyd's system, being a senior meant something. He always gave the more seasoned players a longer leash and greater opportunity to earn a spot on the field, because you earned Boyd's respect over the previous three years of buying into his way of doing things.

But when we had a new coach in 1992, he blew the above plan right out of the water, and I became frustrated—immensely frustrated. And I lost my self-control many times that season. Say it with me, "Son, make the adjustment!"

But I didn't make the adjustment that year. I resisted this change, hard. This new coach valued speed (which I never had). It felt like he couldn't care less about the seniors or, even worse, hated us. In hindsight, it wasn't personal. It was just this new coach's philosophy, and the younger players bought into it. I look back on my senior season at Rollins and have regrets because of how I acted. I used to blame that new coach. Now, I blame myself for reacting the way I did.

From an EQ perspective in hindsight, I was self-aware enough to know I was frustrated. But I lacked composure and self-control in those moments and regretted my actions. I didn't enjoy my senior season as much as I should have. Candidly, I'm a bit embarrassed to admit it took me over thirty years to come to this realization. But again, the lesson for you is that EQ can be learned, and this is just one candid example of it.

PERSONAL AND PROFESSIONAL LESSON
Once you become truly self-aware and have mastered self-control, the final two components of emotional intelligence include social perception and social effectiveness.

Social perception is what other people see in you, how they feel about you, and their perceptions of you. The key word here is "perception," because it isn't necessarily reality. But perception matters in the vast majority of your relationships both in your personal life as well as in your career, so in fact perception is your reality.

Think about it. If you want a raise at work, your boss or other supervisors will consider your perceived value if they were to give you a raise. If they perceive your value to be favorable, you have a good chance at that raise. But if they do not perceive you to be any more valuable than someone else they could hire for the role, your chances aren't particularly good.

When pursuing a personal relationship, let's say someone you want to get married to, they too are also calculating the perceived value you bring to the relationship over the long haul. Most of the time, it's best to have complementary skills with the person you are about to spend the rest of your life with so you can offset each other's weaknesses.

Let me share my own personal and professional ah-ha moment when I finally understood what social perception means and why it's important. This is the story from my previous workplaces I shared in chapter 2, when I had three different 360 reviews over two decades saying I "wasn't a good listener" in 2005, 2016, and in 2023.

Social perception matters because if my boss or the people I work with did not think I was a good listener, there was a strong possibility I didn't get that raise or promotion I was hoping to get at those times. Whether we like it or not, people talk at the water cooler, and how they perceive you matters both in and out of the workplace.

Then comes social effectiveness, which is your ability to get others to do the things you ask them to do, even if they don't report to you or don't have to do it. "The concept of social effectiveness tends to be explained in terms of an individual's ability to identify, comprehend, and attain effective social networks that can produce advantageous career and life outcomes."[4]

A few components of social effectiveness include our ability to influence others, resolve conflicts, manage relationships, hold others accountable, and manage our ego. Anyone in a leadership position must have strength in all of these areas. This includes leadership roles both in and out of the workplace.

Let's use a more common, out-of-the-workplace example of this. More than ten years ago I was the president of little league baseball. In this role, we had more than four hundred kids in the program, sixty coaches, more than a dozen umpires, and over one thousand parents. A typical day at the ball field would include getting the fields ready along with other volunteers, making sure the schedule was accurate on the website and checking the weather forecast. But the number one thing I spent most time on was dealing with people.

One day after a game, we had a coach who was heated about the so-called bad umpiring that caused his team to lose a game. He came charging up to me in the parking lot—this man was a big guy, well over three hundred pounds—and got in my face about what I was going to do to discipline the umpire. (Keep in mind I was not watching the game at the time, so I never saw what he was complaining about.) Additionally, many parents from his team were watching and listening to this interaction.

I listened carefully, didn't overreact, and let him vent.

When I sensed he was about done with his rant I simply asked, "Is there anything else you'd like to share before I respond?"

He said, "No, that's about it."

I responded by saying, "I'm glad you came to speak with me about this, and I want to investigate this further. Right now, emotions are running high, so I would like twenty-four hours to look into this and get back to you. I promise to speak with the umpire, the other coach, and a couple of parents to get their take on this. Will that work for you?"

He agreed, and we walked away.

Upon further investigation, the umpire admitted to missing a couple of calls at key times in the game and said, "We are all human and make mistakes. I'll consider it to be a learning moment, and I will close the loop with the coach."

Upon calling the coach the next day, he was completely calm and much more understanding of the situation. And the matter was closed.

The lesson to learn was that in that moment, one tactic of conflict management I used was to buy time. I just listened with the intent of listening and not responding. I checked my ego and made sure the coach understood I wanted the best possible outcome for everyone involved, given the circumstances. I "influenced" him in the moment to allow me the time to investigate. He didn't have to stop venting. He could have gone on all night.

This also goes back to the one by five principle I referenced earlier: spending one period of time identifying the problem and five times longer solving the problem. I spoke with that coach for about ten minutes and spent about sixty minutes investigating, solving the problem, and closing the loop.

ADJUSTMENTS TO MAKE

1. You must be self-aware in the moment things are happening.
2. You must then have self-control, which is to say you stay in control of your emotions in the moment something is happening.
3. Understanding your emotional triggers can help you improve your self-control.
4. Self-control is a superpower once you master it.
5. Understand the common factor in any of your poor relationships is you.
6. You cannot control other people, but you can influence the way they think.
7. Understand intent versus impact. It's not good enough to say you were well-intentioned. If your words or actions impacted the other side negatively, it's up to you to make the adjustment.

CHAPTER 7

Goal Setting and Making the Adjustment

As you embark on any type of change, you will be confronted with obstacles, setbacks, naysayers, and perhaps the greatest challenge of all: you and your own mindset believing that positive change can happen.

Many times, people convince themselves before the journey even begins that what they are trying to achieve is not possible. But we can't listen to that voice in our head. We need to eliminate negative self-talk and eliminate the words "can't," "don't," and "won't" from our vocabulary. We have to be fully committed and understand our greater purpose and *why* we are changing and setting a new course.

So far in my coaching business, I meet with two distinct types of people.

1. People who are stuck and know they need to make a change, but they are afraid to change or have other

variables prohibiting them from "making the adjustments" needed in their business. Their concerns aren't as much around the cost of executive coaching or training. Rather, they either can't get approval from their boss or board, or it's a family business and they fear the change will have a negative impact on other members.

While I can empathize with their concerns, business leaders have to look out for their clients and business first and their own personal interests second. There's a phrase that it's not show *friends*, it's show *business*! The business has to come first. Business decisions must go in order of doing what's right for your clients, company, and then employees, in that order.

2. The second group of people are most commonly ready to make the adjustment. They are stuck, and clearly something has to change. These engagements are the best types because they've already come to the decision that change is a necessity for improvement. It's just a matter of selecting the right partner.

   In a *Forbes* article on the value of executive coaching and leadership training, Robert Matuson states there's a 788 percent return on investment (ROI) when you hire the right executive coach, which I have seen to be repeatedly true.[1]

With all of that said, if you are on the fence as to whether or not you should hire a coach, I have a few questions for you. What happens if you don't make a change? What happens if things stay the same? Oftentimes after truly asking yourself these questions, you realize regardless of intentions or reasoning, you still are not where you want to be in your business or personal life. This question causes us to come to the reality that you are the one in your own way, and for many people that's a tough pill to swallow. But it's time to swallow this pill with humility, because making a positive change isn't about boosting your ego. It's about knowing you need to change your outcomes and results.

Realizing you are the reason the goal wasn't achieved, or that you are the reason for negative outcomes, is humbling. But you cannot rebuild or reset until you come to that conclusion on your own, or someone helps to get you there. When you build a house, you don't start with the roof or the finish work, you start with the foundation. From here we will start building from the ground up. Great leaders don't manage people through change; they lead through it.

So here's our first chapter exercise. Let's start with scrapping your old goals or business plans. Put your old way of doing things to the side for a minute. Then find a blank white board with dry erase markers preferably. Otherwise, a blank screen or a blank piece of paper will suffice. I want you to write down the number one reason you or your business is stuck or what you'd like to change. This exercise shouldn't take more than a minute.

Then, write down how long you've had these negative results. Has it been three months? A year? Multiple years? Even though you may have had this issue or challenge for years, the good news is you can get unstuck pretty quickly, but only if you are ready to truly change! I know this to be true: It takes twenty-one days to make or break a habit, but it takes six-plus months to change a behavior.[2] And thankfully, via all the data on emotional intelligence, humans *can* change their behaviors with effort, focus, and most importantly, accountability.[3]

I want you to write down your long-term (a.k.a. dream) goal in one to two sentences. Write this in a manner where even a ten-year-old could understand it. When setting goals, I've always advised the SMART approach, as goals need to be:

- Specific,
- Measurable,
- Attainable,
- Relevant, and
- Time bound.

SMART Goals Are...

Specific ✓

Measurable ✓

Atteinable ✓

Relevant ✓

Time-Bound ✓

SMART Goals

I've followed the "less is more" mindset when setting goals thanks to a book called *The 4 Disciplines of Execution.* You will have a far greater chance of success in achieving goals when following the four disciplines to a T, as I've done while running my business along with other businesses I've advised or been responsible for.

The four disciplines include:

- Focus;
- Leverage;
- Engagement; and
- Accountability.

When it comes to focus, the book references having one, but no more than two, "wildly important goals" (a.k.a. WIGs). This creates an intense focus on fewer goals; therefore, we are less likely to be distracted.[3] Many people fall into the trap of doing too many things at once. They chase squirrels all day. These people seem to stay busy all day, yet when we measure what was accomplished, it wasn't as much as we think.

My belief is that over the past number of years in corporate America, multitasking became a skill people seemed to glorify or be proud of. Throughout my time as a business leader, I have found "single tasking" far outweighs the effectiveness of multitasking. How can someone get a dozen things done at once when they can't even focus on one thing for more than five minutes? Later in the book, we will dive into the concepts of time boxing and time blocking, but for now let's stay focused on the task at hand: our long-term, wildly important goals.

In business, what are your goals? Do you want to eventually sell your company? Gain market share? Hire one hundred employees in the next twelve months?

What about your personal life? Do you want to lose weight? Improve a relationship? Save more money?

It doesn't matter what the goal is, just write it down. But whatever you do, *do not have any boundaries or obstacles in mind.* We will get to the detailed plan later. Starting with a clean blank piece of paper or white board is meant to put your mind in a place where there aren't any obstacles. Nothing is limited, and there are no budget restrictions. There's no one in our way except ourselves and our own infinite thinking. So think big. Ask, "What could I accomplish without boundaries?" This is the art of manifesting your outcomes.

Once you have your one or two (but no more than two) goals of what you want to accomplish, start to think about what needs to change for you to accomplish those goals.

When business planning, I recommend something as far-reaching as a ten-year objective, then frame your goal in three years, then one year, then quarterly, and then the next six weeks to start in the direction you want to go.

In your personal life, ask what your "dream goal" is. Then ask how long you realistically think it will take to achieve it. Start to create shorter term goals (similar to the approach in the above sentence) to get started.

One of my mentors and past managers whom I've referenced previously, Bob Dickey, was the president of Randstad Technologies at the time and helped me with what he called the "KDDDA" exercise. He said how too often, we get stuck in "the way we've always done things," and once a month but no more than quarterly, he would *keep* what was working well, *drop* what wasn't working, *delay* less urgent tasks for the important ones, *delegate* more tactical tasks to other staff so he could focus on more strategic work, and *add* the new and innovative ideas.

Speaking of past managers and mentors, another leader who taught me a lot about planning and getting results was the former CEO of Randstad North America. After sixteen years of working at Randstad Technologies, the company brought her in as our new CEO from Canada to run the North American zone. She was a Mensa-level genius, and in my career up until this change, I had always worked for leaders who ran businesses built on relationships, trust, sheer drive, determination, and gut instinct. Yes, we always had a strategy. But along the lines of the book by Jim Collins, *Good to Great*, these leaders believed if they got the "right people on the bus," as Collins stated, almost everything else within the business would take care of itself.[4] And it very much did for those first sixteen years of my career. Our company was highly regarded as one of the top three information technology staffing and solutions companies in the United States and began expanding across the globe through organic growth and acquisitions.

With that growth, our new CEO took on the task of systematizing certain business processes that could be "copied and pasted" across multiple countries. She was seeking a people-focused leader who had both the cognitive ability and experience to define the best practices of hiring, training, and developing individual contributors. She was also seeking a leader who had the experience to define and implement the best practices of hiring, training, and then identifying the high-potential employees and future leaders who could become a core part of our team whom we did not want to lose.

So she began searching internally and externally for the right person for this role. My boss, Bob, pulled me aside one day to tell me the CEO was seeking an executive to lead this initiative. However, even though he recommended me for the role, I wasn't strongly considered due to my lack of professional experience in human resources.

After her first five interviews, she still hadn't identified the right person, and I was finally asked to hop on a plane to Atlanta to interview. This role I was interviewing for was the vice president of growth strategy and development. I asked Bob and others for any advice when interviewing with her, and all they said was, "Don't start with niceties. She's going to get right to business, so have your facts, stats, and data ready to go," which I did. They also said if it goes well she would end up asking more personal questions to get to know me. And that's exactly how the interview went.

But an epiphany around my lack of self-awareness occurred during my interview when she asked, "Chris, your division has the lowest voluntary attrition, highest percentage of people going to President's Club, and one of the highest promotion rates within the company. Your team also has the highest employee engagement scores. How did you accomplish all of this over the past three years?"

The first ten to twenty seconds of my answer likely wasn't that impressive, because I was caught off guard and fumbling through it. I never really thought about *how* I operated as a leader or *how* we got those results. In all those years, I just emulated my bosses and ran the playbook they ran. Which was to say we had a strategy, wrote an annual business plan with clear goals, hired great people, built trust and connections with them, worked hard, and executed our most important tasks to accomplish our goals.

As I was talking through the answer, it started to come to me. I did have a process, but I just never documented it. I never really thought of it as a process. It was just me being me.

But when you work for a company with thirty-five thousand employees at the time in over forty countries, they find the "right person for the right seat" and build out what they called a "best concepts team," and I became part of this team. This is just one reason why Randstad is now the number one HR services company across the globe.

So I ended up being the right person in the right seat at the right time and earned this opportunity to build out a process to:

- Interview and hire talent;
- Train and develop talent;
- Identify internal talent and promote to the next level; and
- Retain talent.

My first order of business was building my own team. I needed the best talent acquisition partners, the best trainers and teammates who shared my core values to build deep connections with our employees to help them achieve their goals, which would help the company achieve its goals. This role was one of the most rewarding ones I had in corporate America, because the company further invested in my own development in the areas of:

- Corporate strategy;
- Workplace culture;
- Instructional design;
- Adult learning;
- Facilitation and content development; and
- Cross-cultural training.

With that, my first project, a plan to lower companywide voluntary attrition while increasing new employee productivity, was approaching. After two weeks of planning, I knew it would take about four months to hire my team and create the content needed for our new training programs. When I presented my plan to our CEO, the first thing she said to me was, "Looks great. Just get it done in two months, not four."

My response was, "I'm not sure that can be done. I thought of every detail and need four months to execute this plan."

Wherein she said, "You haven't asked me the question you should be asking me."

As I scratched my head, I humbly asked, "What's the question I should be asking you?"

She replied, "You haven't asked me if you can get additional resources to help. So if I get you some help, could this be ready in two months?"

My answer, of course, was yes.

This was my first lesson in needing to have an internal locus of control. This concept of locus of control was very new to me, but it changed my life both in business and in my personal life once I discovered and adopted it.

She explained that someone with an "internal" locus of control believes things in their life happen directly because of decisions they make or don't make; things they do or don't do. Those with an "external" locus of control often blame external factors like market conditions, the weather, or other people and essentially make excuses for the bad things that happen in their life or in their business.

Boom. My mind was blown. That day I learned to take full accountability for all the outcomes in my life both at home and at work.

She said, "Chris, the good outcomes you have, and the bad outcomes you have, are due to what you do or don't do. So don't restrict yourself to linear thinking when it comes to problem solving. I need you to think outside of the box to get the results I need when I need them."

This coaching was transformative for my mindset. As someone with a bachelor's degree in mathematics and business administration, I always thought of myself as a strong problem solver, strategic thinker, and systemic thinker. But she inspired me to not limit myself or to make excuses why things didn't get done. "Find a way" was the new mantra and is in-line with what I've observed in the most successful people. They don't make excuses; they get creative and find a way to win and succeed.

ADJUSTMENTS TO MAKE

- Eliminate the words "can't," "don't," and "won't" from your vocabulary.
- Successful people welcome and lead change.
- Successful people don't limit themselves. They are creative, think big, and figure out the details later.
- Adopt a monthly or quarterly KDDDA exercise: What will you keep, drop, delay, delegate, or add?
- Adopt an internal locus of control at home and at work.
- Don't make excuses—ever.

CHAPTER 8

Relentless Persistence

"If you think you can't, you won't. If you think you can, you will."
—HENRY FORD

I've been extremely fortunate to spend time around many greats both in athletics and in the boardroom, including global icons in sports, top producers in business development, and global CEOs. I've met two of the world's 250 wealthiest people. I have been on the field and in the gym with Michael Jordan, Derek Jeter, and Bo Jackson, to name a few. I've also spent many days in board meetings with global CEOs who run multi-billion-dollar companies. This chapter is all about my discoveries when it comes to the commonalities of these people and what's led them to successful outcomes.

Any curious person should always ask what makes great people tick. What are the common attributes? What makes them unique? Out of all the millions of people in the world, how did they make it to the top 1 percent of the top 1 percent in their chosen field? As a curious learner and someone who is constantly seeking ways to improve, I've consistently asked myself these questions.

It's important to have a growth mindset, read or listen to books, and take as many assessment tests as you can to increase your own level of self-awareness and EQ. Too often assessment tests highlight negative traits more so than positive ones, until I discovered one called the StrengthsFinder assessment test by Gallup, which I referenced StrengthsFinder in chapter 2.[1] This test highlights your top five strengths. Mine were:

1. Individualism
2. Strategic
3. Arranger
4. Learner
5. Ideation

When it came to my top trait, individualism, my CliftonStrengths report stated, "Your individualization theme leads you to be intrigued by the unique qualities of each person. You instinctively observe each person's style, each person's motivation, how each thinks, and how each builds relationships. You hear the one-of-a-kind stories in each person's life. This theme explains why you tailor your teaching style to accommodate one person's need to be shown and another's desire to figure it out as they go."

Ah-ha! This explained a lot about why I've always enjoyed the unique traits of each person, helping them grow, and building highly functional teams. It also explained my desire to learn new things and curiosity and excitement to try new ideas.

When it comes to this concept of individualism, I've always had this strength. So I began to wonder what strengths the most successful people had. Based on researching countless articles and interviews, here's what I believe their common attributes, traits, and competencies to be for the most successful people in any chosen field:

- Persistent
- Courageous
- Optimistic
- Results orientated
- Disciplined
- Strategic

Let's start with persistent, or relentless persistence. My old boss, Bob Dickey, had it, and he had a fantastic way to frame it. He would say, "Chris, if you want to be successful in any walk of life, you'll need to have the three Ds—drive, desire, and determination." In a book about behavior change and instilling the proper mindset for success, there's no better example of someone who has this relentlessly persistent mindset than Bob.

I went to high school with his wife, Tracey, and we were good friends growing up. After my four-year stint in professional baseball, I returned home initially working as a bartender and also at a retail store selling computers while trying to figure out my career interests.

One day, Tracey walked into the store with Bob, whom I had only met a couple of times before that day. My initial interactions with Bob were at family events, having a couple of beers and laughs at holiday parties. He struck me as humble, funny, very down to earth… just an overall good guy who I enjoyed interacting with.

After our interaction, on the way home Bob asked Tracey if she thought I'd be interested in working for him at his company, as he was about to be promoted into a management role. Little did I know how intense he was, and I found out when I took my first job with him!

Because Bob had been in sales but hadn't ever managed before, I was the first salesperson he ever hired. I was lucky to have him as a boss, as he became much more than that as a coach, mentor, and friend. He was always tough on me, but I knew it was coming from a good place because I trusted Tracey, which led me to trust Bob. He constantly challenged me to improve. We grew up in the company together, and about every three years we were both earning promotions and additional opportunities thanks to Bob building a talented team and developing his entire staff so well.

There were many meetings where Bob would reference the three Ds. He was always looking to hire, train, and develop his people to have these attributes, knowing full well that if everyone on this team had these competencies and traits, we would find a way to win, which we did. Bob also frames the three Ds around something he would call the "extra one degree."

One time during a leadership conference, he showed a motivational video and asked the audience, "What's the difference between 211 degrees Fahrenheit and 212 degrees Fahrenheit?"

Someone finally spoke up and said 212 degrees Fahrenheit is when water boils.

Bingo.

Bob went on to say, "Exactly. At 211 degrees the water is really hot. But at 212 degrees, boiling water can power a steam engine. And that's the difference between good and great, or failure and success in many cases." He would challenge me to give that little extra effort each day, that extra one degree.

PROFESSIONAL LESSON

Drive, desire, and determination, or in a single phrase "relentless persistence," is one of the most important traits to look for when hiring prospective employees. Those who will persist when things get hard; those who won't quit when the going gets tough; those who won't give up no matter the circumstance and come to work the next day with a fresh mindset that good things will happen—those are the people I want on my team, and you should too.

This leads to a style of interviewing that Bob and I learned together called "behavioral interviewing," which helped me go from saying "I think this person has this trait or doesn't have this or that" to "I know this person has this trait or doesn't." When I coach leaders, my advice is to think about the five or so competencies they need their employees to have. Once they have those competencies locked in, ask open-ended questions of the prospective candidate to tell a story that will explain whether they have that competency or not.

I first began behavioral interviewing almost twenty years ago when I interviewed a young woman who recently graduated from college. She was interviewing for a role in sales and had a background in literature. When she walked in, she came off as bubbly, friendly, smart, and a genuinely nice person. But my initial impression was she probably wouldn't be fit for the role, as I didn't believe she would have an elevated level of relentless persistence when it came to the rigors of a sales career. One of my best employees referred her to me, so I remained open-minded that she might surprise me in the interview, which she eventually did.

Most of my first round interviews last one hour. I spend the first five minutes with niceties then the next ten minutes framing the role and my expectations. I spend the next thirty minutes asking open-ended questions about the key competencies I am seeking. But when it comes to relentless persistence, I never ask, "Are you a persistent person? Do you give up easily?" These are terrible yes or no questions, as almost everyone would say, "Yes, I am hard working," "No, I don't quit easily," and so on.

Rather, what I do is ask the candidate to tell me a story, and I say, "Tell me a time you had some adversity in your life, and tell me what happened." I don't lead them to a successful outcome story. I just state that their answer can be something from their childhood, adolescence, or in their professional life. Through storytelling, you get to see how the candidate thinks, how they handle problems, and what their mindset is. The last fifteen minutes is allowing them to ask any questions they have and schedule next steps from there.

Back to this young woman I was interviewing. We were thirty minutes into a sixty-minute interview, and my gut was telling me she wasn't a great fit for the role. But I stuck to my process and got around to asking her, "What has been the greatest challenge in your life thus far?" I stopped talking… and she puts her head down.

But she wasn't putting her head down because she was lost or seeking an answer. She had an answer. And in the moment I could sense she was getting emotional. So before she spoke I said, "I don't know how deep you would like to go with your answer, and I want you to feel comfortable and safe with whatever you tell me. Because if we are going to work closely together it's probably better we are completely honest with one another right up front. I really am just seeking to know what makes you tick and what your intrinsic motivations are to succeed, especially when this job gets hard, because it will."

She goes on to tell me a story that she met someone who would end up being her high school sweetheart and with whom she was deeply in love. He was "the one" for her. She went off to college, and he went off to serve his country overseas in Iraq. And this love story ended far too soon when she told me he was killed in combat by a roadside bomb. I was stunned. I couldn't believe my question brought us to that place, yet there we were.

Her despair, sadness, and depression were obvious from what she experienced through such a sudden and unexpected loss, but as she fought through tears, this became a story of strength as to what she did to deal with her pain. While mourning, she still went to class, grinded through the most difficult pain she may ever endure, and graduated magna cum laude from a prominent university.

Chills.

For me, at that moment, the interview was over. Not only were we both crying, but she was getting a job offer. She didn't have the experience, but I was always taught as a leader to "hire for character and train for skill." And this young woman had character, lots of it. After I hired her she was wildly successful, and we became close. I will always have a special place in my heart for her and will always look after her as one of her mentors, and she will always be someone I admire for her courage, bravery, and optimism even during the most challenging time in her life.

You see, people who don't quit always win—always. They either lose something and learn from it, or they prevail. Learning is winning. Prevailing is winning. And the road to win is often a long one. So when it comes to the greats, the people who we consider to be successful, it's not always the end result but the willingness to persist when things get tough, whether it is a business challenge, an athletic challenge, a mental toughness challenge—pick any. I would take a team of ten less skilled people with a mindset of relentless persistence versus the team of ten others with raw talent but a weak mindset when things get tough.

The key lessons here are not to quit and to get up when life knocks you down.

If you've never read the book *Outliers* by Malcolm Gladwell, I'd suggest you do.[2] In chapter 2, he introduces a concept called "the ten thousand-hour rule," which states that it takes ten thousand hours of practice to master any skill. Gladwell uses examples like the game of chess, or The Beatles or Mozart to illustrate the rule and argues that success requires time, skill, and luck, as opposed to just natural ability. He further states that coaching and feedback is also paramount to the ten thousand hour rule. It's not just the ten thousand hours you put in. It's the quality of the hours and the subsequent incremental improvements you make through whatever feedback loop you are using.

In my lifetime, I've logged over fifteen thousand hours playing baseball, twenty thousand hours in business development, and thirty thousand hours in leadership and coaching. I've worked incredibly hard to master the only true career interests I've ever had, which were baseball, sales, leadership, and coaching.

Oxford defines persistence as firm or obstinate continuance in a course of action despite difficulty or opposition. Never quitting and putting in the ten thousand hours, especially when faced with obstacles or setbacks, is what relentless persistence is all about.

ADJUSTMENTS TO MAKE

- Relentless persistence is all about your mindset.
  - If you think you can, you will, and if you think you can't, you won't.
- Understanding your strengths will lead to a better mindset, improved self-esteem, and more successful outcomes.
- Have a growth mindset. You either win, or you lose and learn.
- The extra one degree of effort is what separates good from great.
- People with drive, desire, and determination everyday are difficult to hold down or beat in any form of competition.
- When life knocks you down, don't quit. Stay in the game and put in the ten thousand hours to master whatever it is you are trying to accomplish.

CHAPTER 9

Handling Adversity

Greek philosopher Heraclitus once said, "Change is the only constant in life."

I believe the second constant in life is adversity.

My late college baseball coach and mentor Boyd Coffie used to say, "It's not adversity that's the problem, it's how you handle the adversity."

The year after the COVID-19 pandemic was without question one of the toughest years of my life. I was switching jobs, getting divorced, and moving into an apartment at the age of fifty. Money was tight. I became depressed, felt alone, and as a result started drinking too much alcohol. I became overweight and was at an all-time low. All of these circumstances essentially added up to most of the top stressors any one person can endure.

I knew it was time to make the adjustment with a hard reset in life—a rebirth, if you will. I started by giving up alcohol completely and recommitted to my fitness routine from my college and professional baseball days. I wanted to look in the mirror and see the younger man I once was: strong, fit, confident, and happy. During that year in 2021, I would sit alone and knew I had a choice to make: get busy living, or get busy dying. John Stuart, referenced earlier in the chapter on owner's mentality, once said, "When adversity strikes, there are two types of people—engaged or disengaged. Which one you are is a choice." So I chose to reengage and start living my life with purpose again.

I then bought a calendar called "My Life in Weeks" with the assumption I would live to age eighty-eight. This calendar has tiny squares to fill out for every week you live and has fifty-two squares per year, with a total of eighty-eight rows. It's a great visual aid and a reminder to live my life with purpose with whatever time I have left. Some people think this calendar is morbid, but on the contrary, it inspired me to start living each week with purpose. And every Friday afternoon, I fill in another square.

One thing I can say with certainty is while I've had setbacks and sadness the last three years, I've had absolutely no regrets.

As I sat there each night alone after my divorce, I was scrolling through social media and came across the story of the Chinese farmer, a parable that tells of a farmer who lives with his father close to the border with the barbarian territories. Without his fault and without being able to influence them, this farmer goes through various situations which all have important consequences for him and his family:

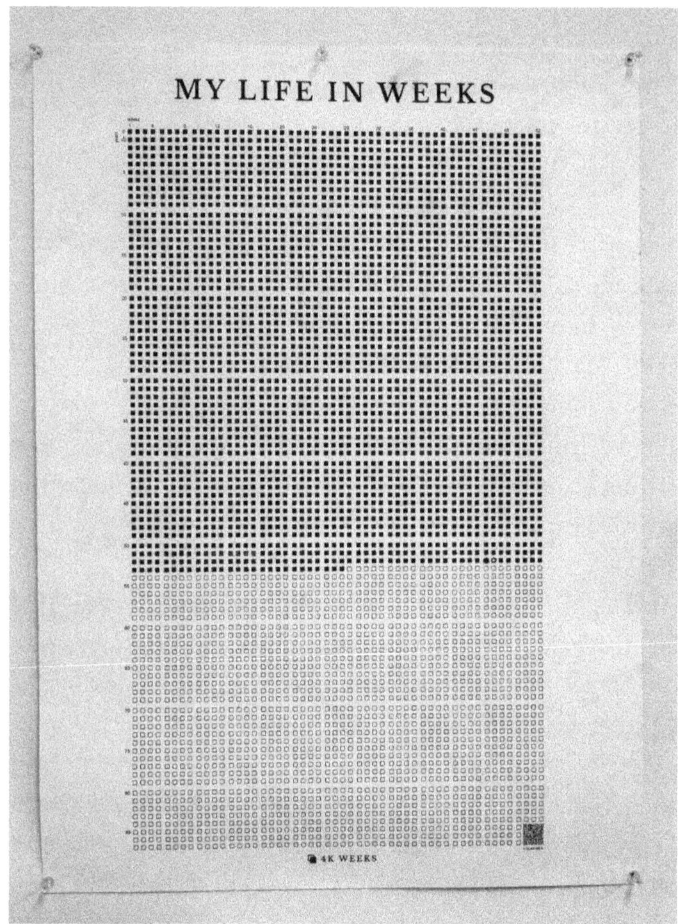

The farmer's horse, a considerable part of his property and livelihood, runs away.

One of his neighbors said to the farmer, "That's terrible your horse ran away." The farmer calmly said, "Maybe yes, maybe no."

After a few weeks, his horse finds its way back and brings along other horses from the barbarian territories, thus increasing the farmer's ability to harvest his crops.

His neighbor was pleased to see the horse come back with even more horses so the farmer could harvest his crops with ease and said to the farmer, "This is amazing. You're so lucky to now have this many horses." Wherein the farmer calmly said, "Maybe yes, maybe no."

Then while trying to ride one of the wild horses, the farmer's son falls and breaks his leg—which reduces his physical capacities.

His neighbor said, "I'm so sorry your son broke his leg. This is terrible. It's going to be almost impossible for him to ride the horses and harvest your crops." The farmer again said, "Maybe yes, maybe no."

Then, barbarians attacked the borderland, and the Chinese Army was unable to draft the farmer's son because he was physically unable to join the battle to help with the defense—whereby he would have likely been killed. Instead, he ends up surviving and escaping death.

The heart of the story was also well framed by the seven-time Super Bowl champion quarterback Tom Brady, who told this story during an interview and said, "We don't have the perspective on what's going to happen in the future. What we may think is good may not be good. And what we may think is bad may not be bad."[1]

We have to keep in mind that all things "bad" may not be bad, nor all things that appear to be "good" may be good. I've since learned the word "maybe" almost always applies in whatever situation you find yourself in.

One could say that being asked to step down at my previous company on April 7, 2023, was a terrible thing. Maybe. I mean, at that moment, it did feel terrible. But I thought, *This seems like a bad thing right now, but it might be a good thing.* By taking things one day at a time, I went from unemployed on April 7, 2023, to making the biggest adjustment of my professional career by opening my business on May 5, 2023. The phone immediately started to ring, and my business closed my first client on May 12. Just like that, I was generating revenue! What felt like an incredibly bad thing became one of the best things that ever happened to me just five weeks later.

When coaching my clients, not only do I know everything written in this book works, I've lived these principles and have proved them out. Only twelve months past that event, what seemed bad at the time has become a great thing. In fact, it may have been one of the best things to ever happen to me. I've learned not to focus on the past and just to focus on the present and future, taking it one day at a time.

While speaking further to John Stuart about this, his advice was to "not to make a bad situation worse. Why would you do that? Okay, you lost your job. Why are you drinking now? How is that going to help? Or you got a bad health report. Now you're eating chicken wings and drinking bourbon every day. Really? But that's what most people do. They make a bad situation worse. Don't do that!"

I'm lucky to have had my fair share of success in my life but also my share of setbacks. I prefer the word "setback" over "failure" because I believe the word "failure" is more permanent, whereas a setback is a short-term loss. But with the right mindset in the long run, a setback becomes a learning opportunity. John once said to me, "I don't know of anyone better than you who can take a beating and bounce back from it with a smile on your face the way you do." I laughed hysterically when he said it as it was intended to be a compliment.

When I think about my setbacks over the past fifty years, if I am brutally honest with myself, I caused many of them. In those moments, I usually blamed external factors, mainly other people. But as I began to better understand the differences between having an internal and an external locus of control, I realized I was the one who caused the setback, even though other people may have been involved. I was the one who needed to be held accountable. It took me many years to come to those conclusions, but the only way we can improve is to admit to ourselves that we need to improve.

REFLECTION POINT

Take a minute to reflect on events in the past where you faced adversity and the outcomes were not what you had hoped for. Then, take a look in the mirror and ask yourself what actions you took or words you said that may have led to those negative outcomes. Chalk this up as a learning opportunity.

A good example of overcoming adversity in my life was after achieving success in the amateur baseball ranks at the high school and college levels. In 1992, the Chicago White Sox drafted me, so I chased my dream of being a major league baseball player and made a good run at it. After some early struggles in my first year in rookie ball, I was assigned to a single-A team in Hickory, North Carolina, in the South Atlantic League in 1993. I played the position of catcher my entire life, and the next big adjustment I would have to make was when the director of minor league instruction informed me, two days before leaving spring training, that I would be playing third base instead of catcher.

I had been a catcher since the age of ten and only played a handful of games at third base at the college level. But Buddy Bell, former big leaguer of two decades, said he would "show me the ropes" and would teach me all the nuances of playing third base in only an hour before we left spring training. He did just that, and off I went to Hickory, North Carolina.

I struggled early on and worked so hard at learning what Buddy taught me at third base. When I say I struggled, I'm probably understating it. I was terrible for a while. One day I walked into the locker room, and my teammates played a prank on me. They removed all the gloves out of my locker and replaced them with frying pans. For about ten seconds, I was mad and embarrassed. But one of my teammates came over to me and said, "Chris, you are one of the best players on our team. You are trying too hard and just need to relax a little. Stop overthinking about this stuff and just react when you are out on the field." That prank loosened me up, which was the exact adjustment I needed to make.

Almost instantly, I stopped overthinking and began to play better. Within three months, I earned South Atlantic League All-Star honors and found myself playing third base next to a future New York Yankees Hall of Fame shortstop Derek Jeter, who was playing for the Greensboro Hornets at the time. That season, I ended up leading the Hickory Crawdads in almost every offensive category during the regular season and played solid defense the rest of the year.

As a result of my solid play, in October 1993, I earned the Chicago White Sox "Minor League Player of the Year Award" and was flown to Comiskey Park to receive it. The first person to congratulate me in the clubhouse was Bo Jackson, legendary two-sport professional athlete in football and baseball, and all he said was, "Can't wait to see you in the big leagues, kid."

Wow. Just wow. I was on the fast-track to the majors… until the next season in 1994.

Only months after that incredible first season in the minors, I sprained my ankle in spring training and was out for six weeks. After vigorous physical therapy, I fought my way back into the lineup as a backup but was no longer starting and/ or a role player. I was frustrated to be sent back to the same team I played for the year before where I was an all-star. But as an eternal optimist, I tried to make the best of it and was "just happy to be there."

When I say that later in life I came to realize I was the one to cause certain setbacks in my life, this story might take the cake. Halfway through the season, I was frustrated and said too much to a reporter from the *Charlotte Observer* newspaper. It was in July 1994, and he said to me, "Chris, you were in Hickory last year, made the all-star team, were the player of the year, and you're back here again. How do you feel about that?"

The first words out of my mouth were something like, "I can't believe I'm still here." The tone was more like, "I can't believe I was player of the year last season and I'm still here. I would have thought I would have moved up to Prince William (middle-A), Sarasota (high-A), or Birmingham (AA) at the very least."

Of course, those comments made their way to the Chicago White Sox front office, and they thought it was me being flippant.

In the baseball movie *Bull Durham*, starring Kevin Costner, Crash Davis gets released from his contract.[2] My same *Bull Durham* moment came after making that comment and was coming back from a road trip from Savannah, Georgia. The whole team was on the bus, and it was 2:30 a.m. I was at the back of the bus playing cards, and our manager, Fred Kendall, said, "Hey Chris, can you get to the field tomorrow around one o'clock? I have something I want to work with you on."

I said, "Yeah, of course. Sounds great," and didn't think anything of it.

The next day, the first strange thing that happened was when pulling into the parking lot, there was only one car (Fred's car). It felt weird. I didn't have any reason to think something bad was going to happen, but it was an eerie, strange feeling.

I got to my locker, and Fred came over and said, "Hey, you got a second?"

I said, "Yeah, sure," and walked into his office.

He said, "Please have a seat, Chris. This is the toughest job a manager has to do. Unfortunately, the organization has made a decision, and they are releasing you from your contract."

I was stunned.

He also said, "It doesn't make any sense to me. You're a good leader, good teammate, and you're playing great, but unfortunately I'm just the messenger here."

I said, "Well, now what?"

"Well, unfortunately you have to pack up your stuff. I know you have your car, so either we can give you money to gas it up to get you home, or we can get you a flight."

"That's it?"

"Yeah, that's it."

I was just sitting there, stunned, but somehow didn't cry. I was just shocked and trying to process what just happened. Then I said, "Fred, I am literally leading the team in almost every offensive category. This makes no sense."

He said, "Chris, I disagree with the decision. I don't know why this is happening. But the organization made a decision, and I have to deliver the message."

And that was that.

I packed up my stuff and went back to my apartment in Hickory. Some of my teammates were there and couldn't believe it either. I slept that night and drove to Prince William County, Virginia, the next day since they had a single-A team there and a lot of my former teammates like Carmine Cappuccio, Mike Cameron, and some others were there. When I walked into the clubhouse, all I heard was, "It's about time you got called up. Let's get you in the line-up."

I said, "No, fellas. I got released." They couldn't believe it either. It didn't make sense to anyone.

I stayed over that night and drove home, but now I was crying through the rest of the ten hour drive back to Tewksbury, Massachusetts. The organization had no money invested in me. They had money invested in other guys at my position and a few others, all of whom made it to the big leagues. It's the business of baseball, and it's really unfortunate. It's not as meritocratic as you would think. It's not the best player who gets the job but more of, "Well, who do we have money invested in?" or "Who does the scouting director feel has the most opportunity to grow into a big leaguer?"

And it's not like they were wrong. I wasn't going to be the next coming of Derek Jeter. I was more of a Kevin Millar, a role player type. I could play multiple positions. I could hit, be good in the clubhouse, was a strong leader, and had many other attributes. But in the White Sox system at the time, they had Robin Ventura, Chris Snopek, Greg Norton, Olmedo Saenz, Pete Rose Jr.... We were stacked, so I don't know what the future would have been like for me.

But my lesson learned in this story, as my Dad once said, "You can't fight city hall." He was right. Later in life I came to find out the director of minor league instruction took my quote in the paper the wrong way, and just cut me loose. In hindsight, without proper context I can't blame him. I've since taken ownership for my behavior. I was just a kid chasing his dreams, feeling like I had been disrespected or wronged. I was wronged, but didn't handle that interview properly.

After being released by the Chicago White Sox in 1994, in 1995 I signed short-term contracts with the Detroit Tigers, New York Mets, and Cleveland Guardians. When my Kinston Indians team won the Carolina League Championship against the Durham Bulls (Yes, the same team as portrayed in the movie *Bull Durham*), I was figuring my last game should be remembered with popping bottles of champagne and the locker room celebration with my friends, teammates, and coaches.

The ankle injury, as well as previous knee injuries, were the catalyst for a series of events that eventually led to my retirement from professional baseball. I came to the conclusion that even though I may have had the skills to make it to the big leagues, the reality was I likely never would, or if I did it would be a long road.

During the long drive home from Kinston, North Carolina, to Boston, Massachusetts, I reflected on the next chapter of my professional life and what it could be. The story of the Chinese farmer becomes relevant again here. Even though I was disappointed with one important chapter of my life ending, it presented an opportunity for a new chapter to begin. Maybe…

ADJUSTMENTS TO MAKE

1. It's not adversity that's the problem; it's what you do (or don't do) to handle the adversity.
2. Use a visual aid each day or week to remind you about your goals and avoid living your life with regrets.
3. Things or events we may think are good may not be good, and what we may think is bad may not be bad.
4. If you've ever faced adversity that led to a negative outcome, be brutally honest with yourself. Take ownership in your role and learn from it.

CHAPTER 10

Being Courageous

———

"What's the worst thing that can happen? And what would I miss out on if I don't even try?"

—TRACI FIATTE

The journey of one thousand miles starts with the first step. I find many times people struggle to take that first step because they overthink their situation, paralyzing themselves due to fear and what could go wrong. Successful people, on the other hand, challenge that way of thinking and get excited about what could go right.

In 2004, while at Sapphire Technologies (later rebranded as Randstad Technologies), after eight years in business development and leadership, Traci Fiatte, one of the senior leaders, tapped me on the shoulder and asked how I saw my career developing in the organization.

Traci had been working as a sales director in New York City, and for anyone who's ever tried to transact business in New York, it is without a doubt the toughest territory in the country. A typical cold call in sales is when you call a prospect and say, "Hello, this is Jim," and quickly go into your pitch. In New York, the most common thing people would answer the phone with was, "Who are you, and what do you want?" At first I couldn't believe it. I thought, *How rude!* But in the Big Apple, time is money!

Traci had grown her career to be number one in sales in the Northeast region and was promoted to director of national accounts due to her skillset of building strong relationships with some of the largest companies in the US. She was hard-working, incredibly intelligent, and seemed fearless, but not in an arrogant way. Traci had a quiet, calm, and confident presence that I admired.

Our company's CEO was looking to promote her to an expanded role, and she had several key national accounts she was personally responsible for in the client portfolio, a few of which I had signed over the previous three years in my role in our Connecticut office. So, she asked if I had any interest in filling her role so she could continue to grow in the organization, which I was excited to explore and eventually accepted.

I worked for Traci directly for a couple of years and learned a ton, and the company had a reorganization in 2006. I ended up working for a new manager, Mark Eldridge, who was another brilliant mind and a great guy to work for. He, too, was highly strategic, humble, and always had an executive presence I admired.

But back to Traci: Her courage impressed me, especially for a demure, female executive growing up in a company that had an 80 percent male executive team at one time.

Over the next ten years, Traci grew her career to eventually lead Randstad North America as CEO with more than $4.4 billion under her management overseeing a more than forty thousand employees.[1] I reached out to let her know about my book and asked where her courageousness came from. Of course, being as humble as she is, she said, "I never really fancied myself this big, brave personality, but I've been told that people think I am courageous. What I realize is it bleeds into the other topic that you referenced earlier, which was mindset. A lot of it is having a positive mindset and knowing, especially as a female in business, sometimes you have to put on courage that isn't really there."

PROFESSIONAL LESSON

She went on to say, "But what I've learned over time is that it's not gender specific. I've learned that men may be better at appearing to be courageous."

When she said that, I remembered a previous Randstad poll where we asked one hundred men and one hundred women if they were ready for the next step to earn a promotion. The poll essentially took two hundred people with similar job titles and production. Wouldn't you know, Traci was right, because 80 percent of the men felt like they were ready, but only 50 percent of the women felt like they were ready. So when I coach female executives especially, I explain that their male counterparts might be raising their hands for a job they are just as qualified, if not more, to do!

When raising my three children (two of which are daughters), I always tried to instill this level of courage and self-confidence to ask for what they want. "You don't get anything if you don't ask," I would say.

Traci went on to apply this type of message to her two daughters as well and said, "I would ask my daughters, ages nineteen and twenty-one, about this. 'What do you want?' I would ask their observations about this dynamic in school. And my older daughter is quite precocious and said, 'When the professor asks a question, the guys just speak up, whereas the girls will raise their hands.' It's funny, right? And so even as elementary, middle school, and high schoolers, you see this dynamic play out where the girls may be a bit more subdued and polite, and the boys are more rambunctious and outspoken. These behaviors start at an early age."

Traci went on to say, "But back to the nuts and bolts of how I either appeared to be courageous to others or brought myself to that point were three things:

"The first thing I would ask myself is: What's the worst thing that could happen? Because the opposite of courage is fear.

And the reason people often aren't brave or courageous is because they're afraid of something. So I would literally go through the practice of saying, 'What am I afraid of, and what's the worst thing that could happen if this goes sideways?' I would literally write down the worst things that could happen.

"There are so many sports analogies about this. As an example, both Wayne Gretzky, the greatest goal scorer in the National Hockey League, and Michael Jordan, the fifth leading scorer in the National Basketball Association, have both said, 'You miss 100 percent the shots you don't take.' So when you reflect on what could go right or what could go wrong, there's a built-in bravery.

"But when I think of being courageous and putting it actually into practice, these are some of the things I would analyze and consider in order to take calculated risks. We've all heard the phrase 'fake it till you make it,' but a better mindset is to take the leap and figure out the things you may not fully know along the way.

"The second thing to consider is: What would I miss out on if I don't even try? There really are some very well-known clichés, one of which is 'name your limitations and they're yours.' And so I believe if you want to, you can. Each day is a choice, and you can choose to be in a good mood and do your best. I believe, at my core, you can choose to be in a good mood. You can choose to eat healthy today. You can choose every single task you do. And I believe that life is a series of choices, and then the consequence of those choices you have to live with, both good and bad.

"The last thing to consider about mindset is to ask if you have an abundance mindset or scarcity mindset. Both mindset and courage are things you have to be very mindful of each day. And this isn't about optimism or pessimism, per se. Again, you can choose, and accomplishing goals takes the proper mindset, discipline, and practice."

Traci believes we all end up becoming, to some degree, a product of our environment. "But it doesn't mean you're stuck there," she said. "You have to push yourself mentally out of your comfort zone. The more you do it, then the more comfortable you become with it, and then it becomes more natural to be courageous." She advises, "You have to be constantly mindful of this and practice in order for it to eventually work for you."

As we kept talking, I told her, "I would imagine one of the biggest fears most people have is looking stupid, right? Most people don't want to look stupid." She agreed with me on this.

I personally experienced this recently. At the age of thirty I learned how to play guitar, at age forty I learned the drums, but at age fifty-three I started taking vocal lessons. During a recent lesson, I was holding back, and my vocal coach asked why. I said, "I feel like I look stupid when I sing."

She laughed and said, "Almost every singer looks silly when they sing. That's why many of them wear sunglasses so you can't see their eyes."

And with that, I started to worry less about looking silly and started to sing better almost immediately. So telling yourself

you can do it is a winning mindset, whereas telling yourself
you can't is the wrong mindset. You have to be courageous
and at least try!

PROFESSIONAL LESSON

I referenced friend and former boss Bob Dickey
earlier in the book, and he, too, carried himself
with a calm, confident demeanor. When it came to
decision-making, especially, there might not have
been anyone better. Bob is the type of leader who,
year in and year out, built tight-knit teams who
routinely outperformed the market by three to four
times whatever that sector was growing.

I had worked with Bob for more than fifteen years,
and right when I think I can't learn something new
from someone I know that long, he once again gave
me some great advice that was incredibly helpful
as a leader.

When I think back on some of the most important
leadership team meetings with Bob, he would walk
out on stage or sit in front of the conference room and
more or less state that we need to adjust our strategy
and make some pretty dramatic changes to evolve.

He would frame his idea and was asking for our
buy-in. Many times these changes were far outside
the box. After the meeting, we would go for a year
executing his plan, and he was always right. He
seemed to see the market one to two years ahead

of everyone else, and we would beat the competition and attain our budget goals.

So a few years ago I finally asked him, "How did you really *know* your ideas and changes would work?"

He said, "I didn't really know. All I could do was evaluate all of the variables, data, and input from others I received. Once I made the decision on what the strategy would be, there was no turning back. That would be the plan, and it wouldn't be up for discussion, and I wouldn't waiver. If you as a leader show any sort of doubt or indecision, it's impossible for your team to believe in you and follow."

While that advice was great, what really helped me in my development was this golden nugget of advice further along in the conversation when he said, "Chris, you probably don't even realize it, but you say, 'I think,' a lot when you speak. And when I hear you say, 'I think,' it implies you really don't know. And that's an area of growth for you: to be less conflicted and more decisive. Your team really enjoys working for you. They are loyal and hard-working, and you're great at coaching and developing them, and they execute.

"But when I bump into your colleagues in the hallway, I get the sense you are too democratic and have a tough time making a firm and fast decision. And as a leader, as much as you need to be open-minded, at the end of the day you are the one who sets the tone, vision, and strategy for your team, so instead of saying, 'I think,' start framing your ideas around 'I know.'"

I *think* versus I *know*. Awesome advice. It was so relevant, because a few years before that, while at an executive development retreat, I was paired up with our CEO at the time, Greg Netland. I had spent a little time with Greg in the boardroom and an occasional round of golf through the years. He was three levels up from my role, so we never really interacted in close proximity. But over the next forty-eight hours, we would both work in a group of six with an executive coach. At the end of the two-day retreat, we were asked to use one word to describe our teammate for the week.

Put yourself in my seat for a minute. I'd been with the company for ten years. I finally got to spend a couple of days with our CEO. We were having deep conversations about our personal and professional development. And I couldn't wait to hear the feedback and the words Greg would use to describe me after having spent the past forty-eight hours together.

The cohort of six people were going around the room, and it was time for Greg to share his feedback with me. The facilitator said, "Greg, based on the past two days spending this time with Chris, what's the word you would use to describe him right now as it relates to his role in the business?"

And he said, "Conflicted." *Huh? What?* In that exact moment, I felt humiliated.

But Greg went on to say, "Chris, you're a smart guy. And I think because you have a high level of empathy for people and see both sides of things, you worry too much about hurting people's feelings. If you choose to be in a leadership role, you'll have to learn that it's better to be consistent than it is to be fair. Because fairness is too subjective. What some people think is fair, others would feel is unfair. Once you establish your principles and what you stand for, you will build greater loyalty and alignment with your team. Sure, some people will disagree, and maybe we part ways with those people, but I would rather have you be more decisive, because more often than not, you will be right. And when you are wrong, just try to be wrong with strategies that carry less risk."

Again, I could go on and on all day about this, but I advise all of my clients (especially early in their career), "Don't pick a job, pick a boss. Because it's hard to find leaders who will challenge you in a positive way and will teach, coach, mentor, and believe in you."

What I learned about courage from Traci, Mark, Bob, Greg, and many other great leaders I worked with is that courage and leadership go hand in hand. Leadership is hard for lots of reasons, two of which are:

1. When you win, you give your team all the credit; and
2. And when you lose, the coach or manager takes all the blame.

You can't be afraid to fail. You need to make the best decisions you can with all the information you have, and as my college coach Boyd would say, "It's not the fear that's the issue, it's how you conquer that fear." Leaders by the nature of the word "lead" go first. Make a decision, show no fear, and move on.

ADJUSTMENTS TO MAKE

1. What would I miss out on if I don't even try?
2. The toughest step is the first step. Take it. What's the worst thing that can happen?
3. You won't get anything if you don't ask.
4. Have an abundance mindset, which is the belief there is enough wealth, happiness, and success in the world for everyone. It's a positive outlook that focuses on opportunities instead of obstacles, and it can help people appreciate what they have instead of fixating on what they lack.
5. If you say the words "I think," it means you don't really know. Put in the work and do the research to know.
6. Be more decisive. If you hesitate, you might allow someone else to make a decision you don't necessarily believe in.

CHAPTER 11

Optimism, Discipline, and Belief

—

"If you don't believe in yourself, who else will?"

I uttered these words three days after losing my job on April 7, 2023. On April 10, I had a choice to make: work for someone else who controlled my future, or believe in myself. Candidly, I wish I had saved more money or had a more detailed plan. And I've always said as an executive that hope is not a strategy. But on April 10, 2023, hope was the strategy!

I had to believe in myself, my work ethic, my experience, and my professional network. I also had to believe I had all the attributes, business acumen, and ability to make the leap from working for someone else to being an entrepreneur at the age of fifty-two. It's one thing in your heart to believe you can accomplish something. And when you have five-figures of debt racked up (and increasing), it's a bit daunting to take on this kind of risk… But this is where optimism, discipline, and belief came in.

Let's start with optimism, and yes, I am that person. I won the "Most Optimistic" superlative award in high school and am not going to apologize for it. I'm not exactly sure where my obscene level of optimism came from, but there are studies that illustrate optimism may be genetic or can also come from the environment in which you were raised. I was lucky to have two parents always instilling in me that anything was possible with the right mindset and work ethic. As an only child, it also didn't hurt that I was told I was special, which I very much believed—until I was seventeen and went away to college and my roommate humbled me considerably!

As stated earlier in the book, I had a quote on my wall in high school that read, "The greatest pleasure in life is doing what others say you could not do." I always loved proving people wrong and took great personal satisfaction in it. Like playing professional baseball during a road game in a stadium away from home, with three thousand hostile fans booing you and cheering for you to fail, then to hit a homerun and the place goes absolutely silent. I loved that silence and proving people wrong.

But throughout my lifetime, I've only had a few dream goals which I am grateful to have attained:

- Goal 1: Become a professional baseball player (goal set at age ten, attained at age twenty).
- Goal 2: Earn $100,000 per year by the age of thirty (goal set at age twenty-six, attained at age twenty-nine).
- Goal 3: Become a C-suite executive running a company exceeding $100 million (goal set at age thirty-five, attained at age fifty-one).

- Goal 4: Start my own company specializing in leadership and sales coaching (goal set at age forty-three, attained at age fifty-two).

Attaining these goals wasn't intended to be self-serving. Rather, it was intended to review how much time it takes to achieve some of your dream goals. Anything great worth attaining isn't easy, because if attaining your hopes and dreams was easy, everyone would do it. This is one reason why I am writing this book. I am trying to illustrate the mindset and, most importantly, document the formula to overcome obstacles, handle adversity, and attain goals, both large and small.

Also note that I had this dream goal in my mind of being a leadership coach more than ten years ago. Yes, I had been a leader and coach in corporate America from 1999 to 2023. But to go out on my own and start a company, my brand, and what I deliver is all on me. This was something I believed I was ready to do because I had the experience. I also believed I had the passion and the X factor, having twenty-plus years of experience running companies but also ten years of experience in adult learning and development. I understood how to create a strategy, but most importantly, I had real-world experience in the trenches. Experience is required to execute that strategy.

Let's define optimism: "Hopefulness and confidence about the future or the successful outcome of something." Author and entrepreneur Justin Prince uncovered that the University of Pennsylvania did a behavioral study over twenty years on 350,000 participants. After studying all of these people, the university researchers noticed a pattern that became predictive of success. One element of that pattern was optimism.[1]

Isn't it amazing that simply having an optimistic mindset and thinking pattern would be predictive of one's success? The study also stated that optimistic people focused on why things were going to work more often than why things weren't going to work.[2]

I've worked with many people who write down their goals or take a picture of a dream outcome. These visual reminders help, especially on the dark days when you aren't in the mood to pursue your goals, which is where discipline comes in. We will get to that later in this chapter.

Justin Prince also found there are two characteristics that optimistic people have:

1. They had unrealistic expectations that they would succeed, which is interesting wording.[3] I wonder if these researchers had a chance to speak with me on April 10, would they have said, "It's pretty unrealistic you're going to pull that off." It's fair to say optimistic people have unrealistic expectations. It's a belief we should stretch to attain what others may believe are unrealistic dreams, unrealistic goals, because the simple pursuit of something great will move your soul. If I pulled it off, you can too. The optimist says, "It's not unrealistic for me. I'm going to make it happen and will prove people wrong."

2. Secondly, optimists kept trying new things until they discovered what worked. The researchers stated, "We don't think you can pull this off," and optimists said, "I

know I can, and I will eventually succeed." Optimists are willing to persist, especially when it gets hard, while others quit, and they are willing to work until success is the only option. Again, remember the *Burn the Boats* reference from earlier: There is only plan A, and plan B is no longer an option!

Another hidden benefit of having an optimistic mindset is that it's good for your health too. In a 2022 study by the National Institute on Aging, findings suggest increasing optimism may be a way to extend lifespan and improve well-being in older adults. Previous research has established that optimism is associated with healthier aging and longevity.[4] Another incredibly gifted author and speaker, Jon Gordon, said, "Optimism is a competitive advantage."[5] I 100 percent agree with him.

This isn't to say that optimists should be wearing the proverbial rose-colored sunglasses and be blind to challenges, obstacles, or reality. I've made a joke as an optimist that we see the glass as half full, the pessimist sees the glass as half empty, but the realist says, "Measure it."

When it comes to mindset, being optimistic has additional benefits. Expert Jordan Peterson said it best when he referenced something he called "realistic optimism" in an interview in 2021. Peterson said, "Humans are wired to over-weigh negative information… We're wired to be more sensitive to threat and to pain… So it's better in some sense to err on the side of caution."[6]

He went on to say, "Go look around and see what needs to be fixed. As soon as you are willing to admit you have a problem (and need to make an adjustment), the act of admitting you have a problem is actually the first step in solving it. And once you admit to the possibility of solving it, that's an optimistic mindset to have."[7] My advice is to never apologize for being optimistic if people can't see what you see.

Another concept synonymous with optimism is "Kaizen," which means "continuous improvement" in Japanese. When I was responsible for training and developing high potential talent while at Randstad Technologies, I would ask other operating company presidents or leaders to come speak to our class. One former leader I worked with, Steve McMahan, was one of those speakers. And one day, he closed a four-day training session with, "At the end of each day, evaluate what went well and what didn't go well. And challenge yourself to become a master of what you do. The top contributors at our company, or any chosen field, are never satisfied. They are intellectually curious and want to get better each and every day. Seek to become a master."

Having an optimistic mindset and attempting to continuously improve is one thing. But you need structure and discipline to execute. So let's dig into that further.

In 2021, I took a Dayforce Leadership assessment test, which stated: "Chris's core conviction is discipline. His discipline conviction means that he is tenaciously optimistic, he loves to get closure on projects. He generally tends to stay the course and doesn't give up until the goal is met or the task is done. Discipline shapes his attitude toward achievement, responsibility, and faithfulness."

So there I was, April 10, 2023, out of a job after twenty-seven straight years of gainful employment. The job market wasn't great, and I didn't want to settle for my next career opportunity. I started to network and speak with recruiters, but I was already feeling I was tired of working for other people and having others dictate the outcomes of my life and career. As soon as I thought those words, I then said, "If you don't believe in yourself to start your own business, who else will?"

And that's when the rest of my career became clear to me. Deep down, I felt in my heart what my "why" and my mission was. Statistically, during my playing days, I was considered to be one of the top one hundred third basemen in the world competing at the highest levels of professional baseball. Professionally, I led a growth strategy team for the number one human resources services firm in the world. I had played and worked with the best of the best. I knew the playbook for success, and now it was up to me to execute and truly make the adjustment. I was a "company of one" and was up for the challenge.

This is where discipline and belief become paramount to success. While responsible for leadership development at Randstad Technologies, I asked every leader to read a book called *The 4 Disciplines of Execution*, written by Chris McChesney, Sean Covey, and Jim Huling. When I first read this book, one of my biggest takeaways was to focus on one, but no more than two, wildly important goals at any one time, because "there will always be more good ideas than you and your teams have the capacity to execute."[8] How often do people make the mistake of chasing ten to twenty goals at any one time and end up achieving none of them?

So my plan was to go to market doing two things, leadership coaching and sales coaching. I was an expert in these areas, and while I also wanted to do advisory work and keynote speaking, I wanted to play to my strengths for what I was known for when starting my business. I knew there would be time to grow into these other areas. Because once I built my brand around my two core offerings (a.k.a. "wildly important goals"), I knew I could set new goals once the first two business lines were up and running full steam.

Jon Gordon once said, "Leadership is a transfer of belief and what your team believes will determine what they create. How a team views adversity and change will define how they grow and who they become."[9] In chapter 1, I referenced my friend and former colleague, Sean Brady, who said something similar: "You can't sell it unless you believe it and are sold yourself." I genuinely believed everything would work out.

And that was me. I believed I could pull off being an entrepreneur for the first time at age fifty-two. I was optimistic. And I would work incredibly hard with extreme discipline. Actor Jim Carrey once said he had "an insane belief in [his] ability to manifest things." He continued, "I believe we're creators. I believe we create with every thought and every word, and every moment is pregnant with the next moment of your life."[10]

I can relate to this because I had an insane amount of belief in myself while playing professional baseball. I was drafted in the second to last round and was barely hanging on to a roster spot. But back in minor league baseball playing days, every single time I stepped up to the plate, I felt like I was better than the opposing pitcher. There were only two at bats in my 883 professional plate appearances when walking up to the plate feeling overmatched. I basically manifested those two negative outcomes as two strikeouts. In the moment I didn't believe I could beat those guys, and I didn't. Yet when I did believe in myself in 1993, I hit .270, made an all-star team, and earned "Single-A Player of the Year" honors.

Interesting how we manifest both the good and negative outcomes, isn't it?

Again, this is why we must eliminate the words "can't," "don't," and "won't" from our vocabulary. If you believe you can, you will, and if you believe you can't, you won't.

ADJUSTMENTS TO MAKE

1. Believe in and bet on yourself.
2. Write down your dream goal and start marching toward it effective immediately. You won't regret it.
3. Being optimistic is good for your health and one's success.
4. Humbly look forward to proving the naysayers wrong.
5. People can manifest the good (or bad) things that happen in their life.
6. Every day is a choice. Choose to live your life filled with optimism, discipline, and belief.

Holding Yourself and Others Accountable

"Expectation management and role clarification have to occur before leaders can hold players accountable. This requires (skillful) communication."

—DUKE UNIVERSITY BASKETBALL COACH MIKE KRZYZEWSKI

Holding yourself accountable sounds easy. As you went through this book, you reframed your new normal and set some personal or professional goals. Perhaps you wrote them down or created a vision board, which I would recommend doing to help manifest your future. But when you are having a difficult day, not feeling well, getting lazy, or losing focus, you will need some help to stay on track.

Earlier in chapter 3, we discussed the importance of shrinking your circle. This chapter helps reinforce one key aspect of why it's important to surround yourself with people you can trust, because these are the people who have the ability to hold you accountable when necessary. I strongly suggest having these people in both your personal and professional life.

A story of this for me starts with my wife, Melissa. After my divorce, I was feeling alone, talking to a mental health therapist once a week, and starting to write down what I looked for in a future partner to support my personal and professional goals.

From our first date, there was immediate chemistry and a lot of laughter. As I got to know her, she was checking a lot of the boxes I was hoping to find in a life partner, which was someone who had similar interests as mine when it came to fitness, open communication, spontaneity, fun, and the three Ds (drive, desire, and determination).

Where the accountability piece became interesting was when Melissa would call me out if I strayed off track from some of our mutual goals, two being a daily fitness routine and healthy diet. In 2022, there was a point in time when I started to get away from eating healthy and was snacking at night or drinking alcohol in the middle of the week, which was something we both agreed we wouldn't do. Then an old back injury crept up on me, and I wasn't at the gym as much as I would have liked. When she first called me out for my actions, I became defensive and essentially shrugged it off. But after a few of these conversations, I began to see she wasn't mad or disappointed in me, she was just holding me accountable to what *my* goals were.

Again, reflecting back on chapter 2, on emotional intelligence, I wasn't truly self-aware of what I was doing at that moment.

But once she helped me become self-aware, my self-control improved and got back on track.

REFLECTION POINT

Have you ever been in a situation at home or at work when someone was trying to hold you accountable, but you really didn't understand what you weren't doing well? I'm willing to bet it's happened to you just like it happened to me. In the heat of that moment, you are on the defense and don't really know how you got here. But you need to truly reflect, without emotion, and be more aware of what is actually happening and exhibit the self-control necessary to get back on track.

When I look back on the setbacks in my life, it's easy to blame external factors or other people. But that's what someone with an external locus of control would do. They would make excuses as to why things didn't go their way. You are no longer that person. You will hold yourself accountable via self-awareness and being truly honest with yourself. I once read a quote that said, "The price of discipline is always less than the pain of regret."[1] No truer words have ever been spoken.

When it comes to your personal or professional goals, what are your expectations? Write them down! Is it behavior change? Weight loss? Shrinking your circle? Getting a promotion at work? It doesn't matter what your goals are; it's important you focus on what you expect from yourself so you can hold yourself accountable if and when you don't meet your own expectations.

Goal Setting

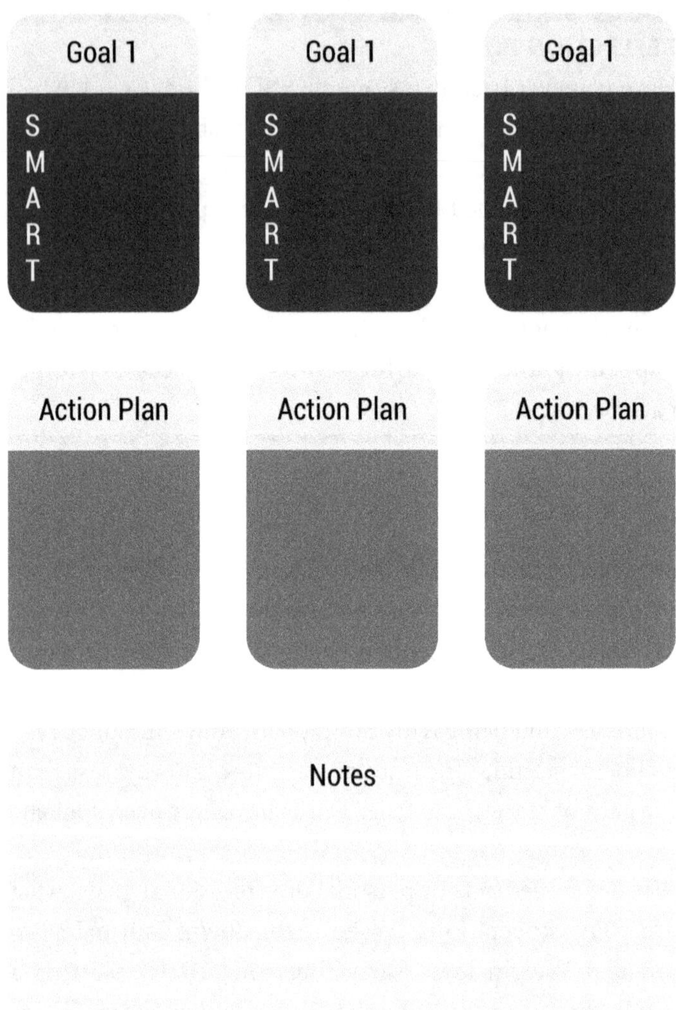

Goal Setting

Another interesting way to view accountability is to look in the mirror and ask yourself if you are meeting your own expectations. When you put your head on your pillow at night, do you have any regrets? Are there things you would have said or done differently? If so, don't beat yourself up over it. Rather, hold yourself accountable to improve the next day with no excuses.

In chapter 9, I shared the "My Life in Weeks" calendar. I've had setbacks and successes, and I have been humbled and enjoyed some wins. But one thing I can say with 100 percent certainty is I've had no regrets—zero. This is the way everyone should live their life.

Jim Carrey spoke about not having regrets at a commencement speech for Maharishi International University in 2014.[2] He framed a story after his dad got fired from his job as an accountant and lost their retirement money as well. His father originally wanted to be a comedian and chose the safer path of pursuing a career as an accountant. Jim went on to say, "I learned many great lessons from my father, not the least of which is you can fail at what you don't want, so you might as well take a chance on doing what you love."

Accountability is hard. It takes a strong person to look themselves in the mirror and be the CEO of their life. The emotional and physical pain is worth it, though, because the alternative is lack of progress or, even worse, failing to achieve your goals.

PROFESSIONAL LESSON

At one point in my life, I played minor league baseball for (eventual) two-time World Series Champion manager Terry (a.k.a. Tito) Francona. When it came to setting expectations via skillful communication, he was one of the best.

A typical interaction when a new player came into the clubhouse (which was me in 1992) looked like this: I was carrying my bag into the locker room, and Tito pulled me aside into his office. His demeanor was friendly and calm yet a confident presence you could feel that he had everything under control without being controlling. He had the ability to disarm you and make you feel comfortable and safe, creating an environment of psychological safety.

I sat down in his office, and he welcomed me to the team and immediately started to explain how things worked, where things were, the schedule, and most importantly, what my role on the team would be. He said, "Chris, you will be rotating with two other guys, and each of you will play catcher; then play third base, first base, designated hitter; then sit out for a game. If at any point this were to change, I will let you know. Every day when you walk into the clubhouse, you know what you can expect. Does that sound good? And do you have any questions?"

After a five minute meeting with him, I felt comfortable, welcomed, and knew my role on the team. As a result, I could start doing my job, get to know my teammates, and go about my business without any head trash on feeling lost, confused, or misunderstanding my role or where I stood. Things were truly clear, which allowed me to be the best player I could be at that time.

Once the expectations were set, I had been playing for a few weeks and vividly remember the day when Tito had to hold me accountable.

I had been in a slump for a couple of weeks and was playing terribly. During batting practice before a game one day, I came into the clubhouse and was cursing at myself or anyone who would even look my way. I threw my bat into my locker and just heard a very stern, "Chris, could you come here for a second please?"

I knew that voice, and Tito wasn't happy with me, nor should he have been. In a very calm yet stern tone he asked me why I was flipping out, and I explained my frustrations around my slump. He listened and simply said, "I think it will be good for you to take a day off and cool down. Your emotions are getting the best of you right now, and you aren't currently able to play your best. Don't worry, you will be in the lineup tomorrow. But it will be best for you and the team to sit out today."

Not only was Tito one of the best baseball strategists I had ever been around, but he was also one of the best managers I had ever been around. I learned so much about baseball and leadership from him. At that time, I was mad not to play that day, but in my heart I knew he was right. And that's what leaders do: They make tough decisions that put the team first.

What's interesting about leadership is the principles are always the same, no matter the industry. Whether you are talking to a CEO, a project manager, a baseball coach, a director of a department… Leadership is leadership, no matter the industry or situation.

Whether you are managing yourself or managing others, my mantra has always been four simple words:

- Set expectations
- Hold accountable

Let's start with setting expectations. Too often, leaders get this wrong. They think they've set clear expectations, but in fact they haven't. You must be crystal clear, because it's impossible to hold others accountable if the goal or what's actually expected isn't completely clear.

One of the best ways to check yourself on this when managing others is at the end of a meeting, close by asking the other person what their takeaways were. More often than not, they will get something wrong, and the first thing I coach leaders on (which was previously referenced on intent versus impact) is, "If the other side doesn't understand the expectations you've set, that's not their fault, it's yours. You weren't completely clear in your communication of what was expected."

If you want to challenge my way of thinking on this, go back and review the chapters on having an owner's mentality and internal locus of control. You must take accountability for your inability to clearly communicate expectations. You can't control other people, you can only control what you say or do.

Be direct. You cannot use soft language or be wishy-washy. Don't sugarcoat what's expected. If someone can't sign up and agree to your expectations, then candidly, they aren't the right fit for your team. We as leaders can never, ever lower the bar when it comes to our expectations. The second you allow mediocrity to creep in, it's extremely hard to eradicate.

You don't have to be mean about this either, just firm. There are many books on effective communication, especially when the stakes are raised. One I often reference is *Crucial Conversations*, where authors Joseph Grenny, Kerry Patterson, Ron McMillan, and Al Switzler talk about being both candid and kind.[3] "Candid" means I am going to shoot you straight. "Kind" means I'm not going to be mean about it and my message is coming from a good place.

Once you feel you clearly communicated expectations, end the meeting by asking the other side what they heard and understood. You can confirm the expectations have been clearly set.

The next piece is to hold them accountable. Let's assume you delegated tasks and set SMART goals or were clear about what was expected over, say, the next week, but said person comes back to you a week later and didn't deliver or meet your expectations. What do you do?

Some leaders would flip out on, yell, scream, or embarrass the employee, which is a terrible option, to say the least. Some leaders would say, "It's okay, no big deal, just do better next time." Again, not an effective way to handle it.

What a leader must do the first time the expectation is not met is be firm, direct, and clear it isn't acceptable. I might say something like, "Okay, for whatever reason, the expectation wasn't met this week, and that's unacceptable. We need to understand the negative impact this has on the team. Everything else we are working on is now delayed due to missing this deadline. What would you suggest we do next time to ensure this doesn't happen again?"

This type of word track has a few elements to call out:

- We've articulated that it's not just about the person who missed the expectation; we articulate how it impacts others.
- The use of the word "we" depersonalizes the conversation. The person on the other side doesn't feel like they are being attacked, because we are attacking the problem, not the person.
- Most importantly, we are setting the tone that negative outcomes are unacceptable.
  - The first time it happens, try to identify if this was a "skill or will" issue:
    - If it was a lack of skills, diagnose, coach, and course correct.
    - If it was a lack of will or effort, give them one warning that this cannot happen again or it would lead to disciplinary action.
    - Fire a verbal shot across the bow so they know you're not pleased and won't put up with missing expectations any further.

Leadership is not for the meek at heart. It's about maximizing the potential of every individual on your team. If one person is capable of producing one hundred widgets, and the other person is capable of producing 130 widgets, hold each person to a standard of what they are capable of achieving. As long as the minimum expectation is being met (a.k.a. one hundred widgets), then everyone is doing their job and being the best version of themselves they can be.

ADJUSTMENTS TO MAKE

1. Accountability starts with setting clear expectations.
2. When someone is holding you accountable, be humble, listen, and check your ego.
   - Remain self-aware and stay in control of your emotions.
3. Don't blame anyone else for where you are or what you've yet to achieve.
4. Take control of your outcomes and don't make excuses.
5. When giving yourself or someone else feedback, be honest, candid, and kind.
6. Set SMART goals (ideally, no more than two or three at a time).

CHAPTER 13

Balancing Confidence and Humility

Playing baseball through high school, college, and at the professional level, you learn that baseball is a team sport, but in many ways it can be an individual one. When you are the one batting at home plate, standing there by yourself with no one else to rely on, it's just you against the pitcher. There's nowhere to hide, and you're very much out there on an island (and that goes for the pitcher too).

As I grew up, I worked incredibly hard on my batting skills and learned a concept called the overload principle, which is to say if the fastest fastball I would see that high school season was eighty-eight miles per hour, I would set the batting machine to ninety miles per hour. If I could hit that, I knew I could hit anyone in the league.

When it came to my level of confidence as a college and professional baseball player, I had it. But that's not the way it always was for me. Early on, I grew up as a slightly overweight kid and lacked self-esteem. I found my confidence through my success in baseball.

With that newfound confidence came a swagger on the baseball diamond. When a pitcher throws a pitch, you have 0.1 seconds to decide if you are going to swing, then 0.1 seconds to swing. If you have any doubt in your abilities, you are toast. I can honestly say I was very self-assured as a batter and was actually a bit cocky.

During my playing days, I believed this air of confidence was necessary to succeed at the most elite level of athletics. Many people told me in my twenties I was cocky. Originally, I wore it as a badge of honor. But as I matured I realized this cockiness wasn't well received by my teammates in sports, in business, or by my friends and family. As I began to reflect, I realized the polar opposite side of cockiness is humility.

When I transitioned away from athletics and started in my first professional sales role working for Bob Dickey, I learned to tone down that cockiness a bit. If I had a good week, I would be strutting around the office like a peacock. One of Bob's greatest one-liners of all time came out when he said, "Good job doing your job. That's why I pay your salary. Now go back to your desk and close some more business." At first I was humiliated, but then I got the joke, and to this day it is one of the greatest leadership one-liners of all time.

Later in life, I was training leaders and sales professionals and met a Navy Seal named Jason Kuhn. We hired him as a keynote speaker, and if you've never spent time one on one with a US Navy Seal, do it. Seek them out and try to spend a few minutes with them. You quickly learn the vast majority of them have the perfect blend of confidence and humility, as Jason most certainly did.

Because I was a coach and trainer, I asked him about the famous BUD/S training that Seals have to endure. He shared that Navy Seals also participated in a form overload training and went on to say, "We believed the training should be far more difficult than anything you would have to endure in combat."

I carry this principle to this day in my corporate training and coaching company. I give leaders and salespeople challenges and scenarios that would be far more difficult than any real life situation they might come across.

PROFESSIONAL LESSON

Bob was the master of picking me up when I was down, but also humbling me when I was a bit too big for myself. And this was the beginning of two especially important traits I found in the absolute best leaders. They were confident but also humble. They had a perfect blend of confidence and humility. Greg Netland, my former CEO, also had these traits, as well as Dan Foley, Mark Eldridge, Traci Fiatte, Bruce Wideburg, and so many more incredibly successful leaders I worked with and directly for early on in my career in business.

They all went on to build $1 billion businesses, and to this day I am so incredibly thankful to work with some of them for more than twenty years. I just assumed all leaders were like them, but later in life found out that more than 70 percent of employees in the US are disengaged in the workplace due to not enjoying working for their direct manager. Which is primarily why the tagline of my business is, "Join us on our mission to create better leaders and sales professionals in this world."

The best advice I can give anyone early in their career is to pick your boss, not necessarily the role, title, or job. When I say pick your boss, the competencies you should be seeking include is to find someone who:

- Is a subject matter expert (in whatever role you are pursuing)
- Has a willingness to coach and develop people
- Has integrity
- Creates environments of psychological safety
- Is empathetic
- Is consistent (creates structure but does not micromanage)
- Is open to learning
- Is innovative

There's some fascinating data around why people leave their jobs, and it is frightening:

- 84 percent of US workers blame bad managers for creating unnecessary stress;[1] and
- 57 percent of US Workers quit specifically because of their boss.[2]

I believe all people naturally err toward one or the other when it comes to confidence and humility, and it takes work to improve the one that is not your naturally dominant trait. In my leadership coaching business, after we complete a 360 review or other personality assessment, I coach clients and quite simply say, "If you're a bit too cocky, tone that aspect of your personality down a bit and be more humble. Talk less and listen more. And if you're a bit too humble, throw your shoulders back with a little more swagger, speak up, and carry yourself with confidence."

The focus is to strike the delicate balance between the two. Like everything in life, never go to excess. Let moderation be your guide.

ADJUSTMENTS TO MAKE

1. In order to improve and be as prepared as you can be, practice and train situations and scenarios that will be harder than what you will likely face in real life.
2. In business, pick your boss, not necessarily the job or role. You will find long term success working for someone who you can learn from and who will challenge you to be the best version you can be.
3. If you're a bit too confident, tone that aspect of your personality down a bit and be more humble.
4. If you're a bit too humble, throw your shoulders back with a little more swagger and carry yourself with confidence.
5. Once you achieve your goals, be proud, but be humble.

Conclusion

To write this book and for you to take this journey with me is incredibly humbling. It's funny, since the last chapter being about the perfect blend of confidence and humility. That was my Coach Boyd Coffie to a T: such a soft spoken yet confident presence; calm yet in command and control, but never overbearing; always pushing us when we needed it and assuring us when we needed that too.

Looking back, I cannot believe how lucky I was to have gone to school at Rollins College and play for him. I'm convinced my former teammates, myself, or anyone who spent a significant amount of time with Boyd would not be where we are in our lives if not for him and the lessons he taught us.

Many years ago, one of my former bosses asked me what my dream job would be. He said, "Let's say you had just enough money in the bank to pay your bills for the rest of your life, but you still want to work because you want to stay busy as a productive member of society. What would you do? What would your dream job be if money wasn't part of the equation?"

I immediately answered that I would want to be a college baseball coach, just like my mentor and coach Boyd. But my experiences over the past three decades were in the business world, and I quickly figured out that being a leader or sales coach was essentially the same thing as being a baseball coach. Instead of wearing a hat and whistle and throwing batting practice, I wore a pressed shirt, good shoes, and a nice watch (thanks for that advice, Greg Netland!).

I'm a coach at heart. That was my dream job. I enjoy using my past experiences, both the good and the bad, and relating these stories to my clients to help them make the adjustments needed in their business or even in their personal lives.

I once read in a *Harvard Business Review* article, "You can't take care of others until you first take care of yourself," and I believe this to be true.[1] I've worked so hard on myself through the years on all the concepts presented in this book. Just like the advice in the previous chapter, early on in my career I was a bit too confident and had to dial up my humility. But even though I worked hard on that balance, nothing in this world will humble someone like losing a job. Especially being a father, a husband, and a provider, it's beyond humbling—it's humiliating when it's a struggle to provide for your family.

I took on well over five figures of debt after losing my job. Even though that caused some stress, the funny thing was I was never really worried. And that's where every single lesson in this book comes in. I knew I had to be optimistic, focused, and, most importantly, disciplined. Because not only have I observed these traits in others, I lived them and was very much forced to in 2023. Not only did things work out, but my life is better than ever.

Earlier in the book I referenced my divorce, and like most people after divorce, I reflected, tried to become a better version of myself, and get "back out there," as they say. Thankfully, I met an amazing woman who became my wife in June 2024, now Melissa Mader. She has a master's degree in education and mental health and helped me tremendously when it comes to so many lessons in this book: self-awareness, humility, belief, loyalty, and support, among so many others, all while having fun along the way. I would not be where I am today without her support.

That's the message I want to close with. Everything outlined in this book is the roadmap to understanding how we as humans react to change and how *we* are in control of the outcomes in our life. *Make the Adjustment* is not only a universal mantra for almost any situation you find yourself in, but making the adjustment is a very personal journey to you and no one else. No one else should dictate your hopes, goals, or dreams. If you are not happy, if something isn't working, my advice is quite simply, "Make the adjustment."

Early on in the book, we introduced the concept of emotional intelligence (EQ) and your level of self-awareness. You must be incredibly honest with yourself as to what your strengths and weaknesses are, and continue to leverage those strengths but also improve your weaknesses.

Then, shrink your inner circle and find the people you want to hitch your wagon with. Meaning, spend your time with those who bring you energy and support you unconditionally. Have the discipline to avoid people who drain your energy or don't have your best interests in mind. With these people, cut ties and cut them out of your life. You'll be thankful you did later.

Remember, behavior change is hard, and it takes twenty-one days to make or break a habit but much longer to change a behavior—more like six-plus months. Once you better understand your propensity and openness to change, you can take on an owner's mentality and start to own your behaviors, habits, and what you say and do each day. I've always said I'm not a fan of New Year's resolutions, because we as humans can choose what we do with our time each day. Why wait until January 1 each year to commit to changing for the better? Start today. That's what an owner would and should do.

Which leads to self-control when things get hard and you're confronted with a challenge or obstacle. Discipline and control come in here. We cannot give in to others who try to derail or distract us. We cannot react in a negative or overly emotional manner. Rather, we must stay positive and committed to our mission of change and continuous improvement and forge ahead with quiet confidence. Add the concept of having an internal locus of control, stop making excuses, and take control of your behaviors, actions, and outcomes.

When obstacles or challenges present themselves, this is when we must stay committed with relentless persistence. As Boyd always said, "It's not adversity that's the problem, it's how you handle the adversity." Your level of courageousness takes over here. Be authentic to yourself, even if that means leaving people behind. Not everyone will understand where you are going, and that's okay. Ask yourself, "What's the worst thing that can happen," and, more importantly, "How would I feel if I don't even try?" Do not live your life with regrets.

Your level of optimism must outweigh all the naysayers and negativity you will encounter. Pay them no mind. You are on your mission. If you don't believe, how will anyone else believe? If you are a leader and don't believe in your mission or vision, your people will see right through you. But once the vision is solid, you need to be disciplined and create the proper structure for yourself and your team. You must have a repeatable, consistent process to follow, especially on the tough days when outside factors try to derail you.

As we near the end of any type of change, now comes accountability. We must set clear expectations and hold ourselves and others accountable. Did we make the right adjustments? Do not let mediocrity creep into your life or business. Continue to challenge yourself and others in a psychologically safe manner. But keep raising the bar and never lower it.

But when you reach the top of the mountain, do so with humility. Be proud. Celebrate with your newly created smaller circle, but don't boast. If you accomplished an individual goal, reward yourself. If it was a team goal, reward the team. Life's too short to not celebrate the small victories and especially the big ones. The best of the best quickly focus on what's next and sometimes forget to celebrate their accomplishments once they happen. So pause for a moment, reflect, drink it in, and enjoy the wins when they come.

The last thought I will leave with you is a relevant analogy which comes from the staffing industry, especially the permanent placement sector. On the first day of each month, we would all walk into the office, and our manager would erase the previous month's revenue results. Everyone's name on the sales board was at $0. Whatever you derived for revenue the previous month was over. We had to rebuild our business on the first day of every month. My old boss Bob always said, "Chris, welcome to the revenue regeneration business." And he would say it with a wry tongue-in-cheek smirk. But he was right. On day one of every month, we all started at zero.

So let's apply that to you and whatever goals you have. Every day, we start at *zero*. It doesn't matter what you did yesterday. Yesterday is over, and there's no guarantee of what you will do tomorrow. The second your eyes open each day, you have control of every single thing you do, everything you say, every decision you make. You start each day at *zero*. This is why we have to apply the lessons discussed in this book. Every day you have a choice: You can get better, or you can get worse.

I hope this book inspires you to make the adjustments needed in order to attain your goals, hopes, and dreams.

If you believe, I believe.

"Live your life filled with optimism, passion,
and purpose… not regret."

CHRIS MADER

April 23, 2023

Acknowledgments

I would be remiss if I did not thank all of the people who made significant contributions to this book and for that matter were a positive influence in my life. I don't even know where to begin, but I will start from my beginnings and work up to the present.

First off, this book is dedicated to my mother. After giving birth to me in 1970, she was incapable of bearing future children, which is an incredible shame because she was made to be a mom. She was the best mother a son could ever have. She did everything to ensure I had a happy childhood, which I very much did. Thank you, Mom, for your unconditional love and support, I would not be who I am today without you.

Next there's my father, who was my father first but then became my best friend as I became an adult. From the age of birth to ten years old, he worked many hours to build his career in sales and own businesses to support our family. He coached all of my baseball teams between the ages of ten to seventeen, and later he became a successful college baseball coach and professional baseball scout in his own right. He won a World Series ring in 2002 as a pro scout with the now Los Angeles Angels and was far more successful as a scout than I ever was as a player. But Dad is a kind, old school type of guy who gave me great advice and always had my back. I could only wish every child had two parents like Guy and Linda Mader.

Then, two of the most formative coaches in baseball I had early on were my high school baseball coach Bob Ware and, of course, my college baseball Coach Boyd Coffie. They have both since passed away but were incredible influences in my life on and off the baseball diamond. In the professional baseball ranks, I want to acknowledge Fred Kendall, Mark Salas, Tito Francona, Buddy Bell, Mookie Wilson, Gordie MacKenzie, Hank Sargent, and Arnie Beyeler, who were great coaches and mentors and supported me. Thank you.

To my wife, Melissa, I am so incredibly lucky to have you as my best friend and true partner to navigate the trials and tribulations of life. Since the first day we met, you've always been there with love, support, and, most importantly, laughter. You're my favorite workout partner and make me a better person each day, and for that I am grateful. I love you.

To our children, I hope this book serves as additional guidance, advice, and best practices on how to overcome obstacles in life, handle the constant world of change, make adjustments, and accomplish goals. Anything is possible once you understand your greater purpose and have a strong work ethic, discipline, and belief. Always believe in yourself, even when no one else will… and your dreams will come true. I love you all very much.

In the business world, many of these people were previously referenced, but I worked with countless pioneers in the staffing industry over the past twenty-five years: Bob Dickey, Alison Cohen, Dan Foley, Bruce Wideburg, Greg Netland, Traci Fiatte, John Stuart, Mark Eldridge, Kirstin Kelley, Sean Brady, Rick Martyn, Brad Page, Richard Zambaca, Greg Coir, Teresa Creech, Steve McMahan, Chris Martin, Ursula Williams, Andy Speer, Alisia Genzler, Steve Brady, Frank Waite, Grant Smith, Brock Bauer, Sejal Shah, Jason Jarrett, Gene Scheurer, and Lydia Veal McRae, to name a few. Your coaching, mentoring, candor, and friendship had an incredibly formative impact on my leadership style and anything I've ever accomplished. Thank you.

A very special acknowledgment to my role model as an entrepreneur and also the founder and CEO of Medicus Healthcare Solutions, Joe Matarese. He not only offered to write the foreword for this book but volunteered his time and energy to review each chapter and provide invaluable feedback to help ensure this book could be the best it could be. Thank you, Joe.

In the tough year that was 2023, I don't think these people realize the positive impact they had on me, especially when times were tough: Lou Longo, Jim Larsen, Billy Irvin, Jimmy Olson, Jason Kuhn, Casey Jacox, Jon Gordon, Dianne Dismukes, Greg Carbone, Jon Lorden, Cheryl Abbott, Karyn Ramey, Jason Posnick, Kirstin Lynde, Doug Hurley, Rob Mann, Lesly Vickrey, and James McIlroy all went out of their way to help and asked for nothing in return. And one special acknowledgment to my former colleague and friend Erin Posnick, as my conversation with you in April 2023 gave me that last bit of confidence, courage, and energy to start my business. Talk about having a great network of smart, caring people looking out for you. I'm so grateful for all of you.

To MTA Consultancy's first clients who included Chris Chausse, Jim Sullivan, George Hotter, Elizabeth Ahearn, Kiley Carlton, Charity Taylor, Kathryn Krueger, John Stuart, Kirstin Kelley, and a few clients who chose to be anonymous (you know who you are), thank you for partnering with MTA and trusting us to guide and improve your business outcomes in 2023, 2024, and beyond.

To Krysta Van Ranst and Paige Garland at Building PPL, thank you for teaching me and my clients about how applying for state grants could earn additional training opportunities and attain better outcomes in their business. MTA Consultancy's success accelerated thanks to our partnership.

To my team at Manuscripts LLC, especially Eric Koester: Thank you for giving me the courage to write a book and creating a process to ensure it could be the best it could be.

A special thanks to my daughters, Brooke Mader, Kate Mader, and Madison Hayward, as well as my first employee at MTA Consultancy, Mackenzie Wakem. Thank you for helping with the research and editing needed during the mad dash at the end of the book writing process.

Lastly, to my teammates from Rollins College baseball circa 1988–1992, all of whom played for Boyd. This book in many ways comes from all of us and those who played for Boyd before us. Together, we got up at 6:00 a.m. and did running drills for an hour, only to go to class, come back to the field in the afternoon to practice for four-plus hours, do the bars workout, and do it again the next day—over and over again. We played our way through the 1989 Sunshine State Conference regionals and made it to the final eight in the 1989 Division II World Series for the first time in school history. That gave us all incredible pride and memories we will never forget.

My journey with my Rollins teammates started freshman year at Elizabeth Hall with my roommate Carmine Cappuccio, along with Fred Seymour, Bill Jacobs, and John Brockett right next door. And the rest of the boys included Dave Ciambella, Keith Jones, Brian Riva, Jim Hahn, Chip Deklyn, Todd Diebel, Darrel Card, Mike Lynch, Clay Bellinger, Mitch Stringer, Ray Fernandez, Jim Barnick, and John Kendrigan.

Before naming my business and authoring this book, I reached out to another special former teammate and Boyd's son, Trey Coffie. I wouldn't have been able to launch MTA Consultancy with our tagline of "Make the adjustment" without his blessing, so thank you for that, Trey, along with your friendship during our time together at Rollins.

Just to think… If Boyd could see us all today, what would he say? I'd like to think he'd be proud we stuck together and that our friendships reached far beyond the locker room, weight room, or baseball field. We're such a diverse cast of characters, but we had a few things in common, which included buying into his system, giving our best effort each day, and always fighting for each other. Without question, we continuously worked hard to overcome whatever challenges baseball or life threw at us. He taught us it's okay to make mistakes, just learn from them, make the adjustment, and move on. We all had no idea at the time that Boyd wasn't just our baseball coach, he was like a second father to us. I'd like to think he's somewhere watching over us with a firm hand on our shoulder, smiling and proud of who we've become and continue to aspire to be.

End Notes

INTRODUCTION

1. Wanda Thibodeaux, "Five Statistics That Will Restore Your Faith in Humanity (and the Office)," *Innovate* (blog), *Inc.*, July 24, 2019, https://www.inc.com/wanda-thibodeaux/5-statistics-that-will-restore-your-faith-in-humanity-and-office.html.

CHAPTER 1

1. Simon Sinek, *Start with Why: How Great Leaders Inspire Everyone to Take Action* (New York City, New York: Penguin Books, 2011), 41–43.

2. Tom Brady, "Tom Brady Opens up—7th Ring Motivation MJ or Belichick | Enemies | Style of Leadership," PBD Podcast, September 20, 2023, 01:42:06, https://www.youtube.com/watch?v=liz8rZx1NJ8.

3. Steve Jobs, "Steve Jobs' 2005 Stanford Commencement Address," Stanford, March 7, 2008, 00:15:04, https://youtu.be/UF8uR6Z6KLc?si=Zyu2_35BhPQNN8Rn.

4. Kobe Bryant, "TEDxShanghaiSalon—Power of the Mind," Richard Hsu, July 25, 2016, 00:42:06, https://youtu.be/9_tYXFbgjZk?si=wEnIaRPm9H6YFURn.

5. Oh No They Didn't! Staff, "Daily Fail Does One Thing Right and Gives Us a Nice Taylor Swift Interview," *ONTD* (blog), February 2, 2014, https://ohnotheydidnt.livejournal.com/85363044.html.

6. Monica Mercuri, "Taylor Swift Didn't Need Lucrative Side Hustles to Become a Billionaire," *Business* (blog), *Forbes*, April 2, 2024, https://www.forbes.com/sites/monicamercuri/2024/04/02/taylor-swift-didnt-need-lucrative-side-hustles-to-become-a-billionaire/?sh=551865934a9d.

7. Mike Tyson, "You Are Nothing without Discipline," Mike Tyson, July 17, 2023, 00:00:17, https://www.youtube.com/watch?v=YW-WBvXH9Ho.

8. Simon Sinek, "Adopting an Infinite Mindset," Simon Sinek, October 21, 2022, 00:00:11, https://www.youtube.com/watch?v=Rh6XLrMK-hg.

9. US Surgeon General, *Social Media and Youth Mental Health* (Washington, DC: The US Surgeon General's Advisory, 2023), 7, https://www.hhs.gov/sites/default/files/sg-youth-mental-health-social-media-advisory.pdf.

10. Fazida Karim, Azeezat A. Oyewande, Lamis F. Abdalla, Reem Chaudhry Ehsanullah, and Safeera Khan, "Social Media Use and Its Connection to Mental Health: A Systematic Review," *Cureus* 12, no. 6 (June 2020), https://doi.org/10.7759/cureus.8627.

CHAPTER 2

1. Finding Mastery, "Emotional Intelligence Is a Superpower," Dr. Daniel Goleman, October 8, 2021, 00:03:30, https://www.youtube.com/watch?v=SXW3XH08G3M.

2. Michael Beldoch, "Sensitivity to Expression of Emotional Meaning in Three Modes of Communication," in *The Communication of Emotional Meaning*, J. R. Davitz et al. (New York City, New York: McGraw-Hill, 1964).

3. Daniel Goleman, *Working with Emotional Intelligence* (New York City, New York: Bantam Books, 1998).

4. David R. Klamm, "No, Your IQ Is Not Constant," *Memory Medic* (blog), *Psychology Today*, May 27, 2018, https://www.psychologytoday.com/us/blog/memory-medic/201805/no-your-iq-is-not-constant.

5. David Goggins, "David Goggins—Get Better Every Day | Powerful Speech," Global Motivation, January 15, 2023, 00:22:56, https://www.youtube.com/watch?v=pp3QXJu1ylo.

6. Daniel Goleman, *Working with Emotional Intelligence* (New York City, New York: Bantam Books, 1998), 25.

7. Tasha Eurich, "Working with People Who Aren't Self-Aware," *Difficult Conversations* (blog), *Harvard Business Review*, October 19, 2018, https://hbr.org/2018/10/working-with-people-who-arent-self-aware.

8. Ryan Holiday and Stephen Hanselman, *Daily Stoic* (New York City, New York: Penguin Random House, 2016).

9. Gallup, "An Introduction to the Ideation CliftonStrengths Theme," *CliftonStrengths* (blog), Gallup, accessed June 20, 2024, https://www.gallup.com/cliftonstrengths/en/252260/ideation-theme.aspx.

CHAPTER 3

1. Ryan Holiday and Stephen Hanselman, *Daily Stoic* (New York City, New York: Penguin Random House, 2016).

2. Aimee Groth, "You're the Average of the Five People You Spend the Most Time With," *Strategy* (blog), *Business Insider,* July 24, 2012, https://www.businessinsider.com/jim-rohn-youre-the-average-of-the-five-people-you-spend-the-most-time-with-2012-7

3. Scott Gerber, "Why Your Inner Circle Should Stay Small, and How to Shrink It," *Professional Networks* (blog), *Harvard Business Review,* March 7, 2018, https://hbr.org/2018/03/why-your-inner-circle-should-stay-small-and-how-to-shrink-it?utm_medium=emailandutm_source=newsletter_dailyandutm_campaign=mtodandreferral=00203.

4. Ibid.

5. Tim Dahi, "Practical Tips You Need to Pick the Five or So People in Your Inner Circle," *Change Becomes You* (blog), January 26, 2022, https://medium.com/change-becomes-you/practical-tips-you-need-to-pick-the-5-or-so-people-in-your-inner-circle-a0e73d883390.

CHAPTER 4

1. Matt Higgins, *Burn the Boats: Toss Plan B Overboard and Unleash Your Full Potential* (New York City, New York: William Morrow, 2023).

2. Ed Sheeran, "Ed Sheeran on the Power of Failure—*The Howard Stern Show*," Jacob Beard, June 2, 2023, 00:03:31, https://www.youtube.com/watch?v=SwegMPrTHBc.

3. Ibid.

CHAPTER 5

1. Philip G. Zimbardo and Michael R. Leippe, *The Psychology of Attitude Change and Social Influence* (New York City, New York: McGraw-Hill, 1991).

2. Wayne W. LaMorte, "Diffusion of Innovation Theory," *Behavioral Change Models* (blog), Boston University School of Public Health, November 3, 2022, https://sphweb.bumc.bu.edu/otlt/mph-modules/sb/behavioralchangetheories/BehavioralChangeTheories4.html.

3. Ibid.

4. Wayne W. LaMorte, "Diffusion of Innovation Theory," *Behavioral Change Models* (blog), Boston University School of Public Health, November 3, 2022, https://sphweb.bumc.bu.edu/otlt/mph-modules/sb/behavioralchangetheories/BehavioralChangeTheories4.html.

5. Ibid.

CHAPTER 6

1. Cary Cherniss, *The Business Case for Emotional Intelligence* (Piscataway, New Jersey: Consortium for Research on Emotional Intelligence in Organizations, 1999), 2.

2. Brian Knight, "The DMGB Mindset: Doesn't Matter, Get Better," *Daily Discipline* (blog), *Brian Knight*, accessed May 20, 2024, https://www.tbriankight.com/blog/dmgb-doesnt-matter-get-better.

3. Wanda Thibodeaux, "Five Statistics That Will Restore Your Faith in Humanity (and the Office)," *Innovate* (blog), *Inc.*, July 24, 2019, https://www.inc.com/wanda-thibodeaux/5-statistics-that-will-restore-your-faith-in-humanity-and-office.html.

4. Marshall Magnusen and Pamela L. Perrewé, "The Role of Social Effectiveness in Leadership: A Critical Review and Lessons for Sport Management," *Sport Management Education Journal* 10, no. 1 (April 2016): 64–77, https://www.researchgate.net/publication/301569286_The_Role_of_Social_Effectiveness_in_Leadership_A_Critical_Review_and_Lessons_for_Sport_Management.

CHAPTER 7

1. Roberta Matuson, "Is Executive Coaching Really Worth the Money?" *Forbes*, July 27, 2023, https://www.forbes.com/sites/robertamatuson/2023/07/27/is-executive-coaching-really-worth-the-money/.

2. Ben D. Gardner, "Busting the Twenty-One Days Habit Formation Myth," *Health Chatter* (blog), University College

London, June 29, 2012, https://blogs.ucl.ac.uk/bsh/2012/06/29/busting-the-21-days-habit-formation-myth/.

3. Chris McChesney, Sean Covey, and Jim Huling, *The 4 Disciplines of Execution: Achieving Your Wildly Important Goals* (New York City, New York: Simon and Schuster, 2012).

4. Jim Collins, *Good to Great: Why Some Companies Make the Leap… And Others Don't* (New York City, New York: Harper Business, 2001).

CHAPTER 8:

1. Gallup, "Looking for StrengthsFinder? You're in the Right Place," *CliftonStrengths* (blog), Gallup, accessed December 27, 2023, https://www.gallup.com/cliftonstrengths/en/254033/strengthsfinder.aspx.

2. Malcolm Gladwell, *Outliers: The Story of Success* (Boston, Massachusetts: Little, Brown and Company, 2008), 35–68.

CHAPTER 9

1. Tom Brady, "Life is all about perspective", TikTok: *alyseanderson21*, January 16, 2022, 00:01:17, https://www.tiktok.com/@alyseanderson21/video/7053853742776503599?lang=en

2. *Bull Durham*, directed by Ron Shelton (1988; The Mount Company, 1988), 01:48:00.

CHAPTER 10

1. Sander van 't Noordende and Jorge Vazquez, *4th Quarter Results 2023* (Atlanta, GA: Randstad, 2024), https://www.randstad.com/s3fs-media/rscom/public/2024-02/Q4_2023_Presentation_0.pdf.

CHAPTER 11

1. Justin Prince, "The Mindset of the 1 Percent," Justin Prince, April 17, 2023, 00:04:40, https://www.youtube.com/watch?v=Sq76RwPKXas.

2. Ibid.

3. Justin Prince, "The Mindset of the 1 Percent," Justin Prince, April 17, 2023, 00:04:40, https://www.youtube.com/watch?v=Sq76RwPKXas.

4. National Institute on Aging, "Optimism Linked to Longevity and Well-being in Two Recent Studies," *Research Highlights* (blog), *National Institute on Aging*, December 8, 2022, https://www.nia.nih.gov/news/optimism-linked-longevity-and-well-being-two-recent-studies#:~:text=Optimism%20is%20linked%20to%20a,to%20two%20NIA%2Dfunded%20studies.

5. Jon Gordon, "Optimism Is a Competitive Advantage," *Pulse* (blog), LinkedIn, January 13, 2020, https://www.linkedin.com/pulse/optimism-competitive-advantage-jon-gordon/.

6. Jordan Peterson, "Realistic Optimism | Matt Ridley and Jordan B. Peterson," Jordan B. Peterson Clips, February 12, 2021, 00:08:09, https://www.youtube.com/watch?v=heqZuvIDo5o

7. Ibid.

8. Chris McChesney, Sean Covey, and Jim Huling, *The Four Disciplines of Execution* (New York City, New York: Simon and Schuster, 2022), 11.

9. Jon Gordon, "How Do You Overcome?" *Weekly Newsletter* (blog), The Jon Gordon Companies, accessed December 6, 2023, https://jongordon.com/positivetip/howdoyou overcome.html.

10. Jim Carrey, "Jim Carrey Talks about His Ability to Manifest Things," *Self-Development* (blog), *Goalcast*, September 14, 2016, https://www.goalcast.com/jim-carreys-talks-ability-manifest-things/.

CHAPTER 12

1. Clyde Lee Dennis, "7 Good Minutes: Extra—The Price of Discipline Is Always Less than the Pain of Regret," 7 Good Minutes, September 26, 2023, 2:20, https://www.youtube.com/watch?v=SsYwUjl5AW4.

2. Jim Carrey, "Jim Carrey at MIU: Commencement Address at the 2014 Graduation," Maharishi International University, May 30, 2014, 12:19, https://www.youtube.com/watch?v=V80-gPkpH6M.

3. Kerry Patterson, Joseph Grenny, Ron McMillan, and Al Switzler, *Crucial Conversations: Tools for Talking When Stakes Are High* (New York City, New York: McGraw-Hill, 2002).

CHAPTER 13

1. Society for Human Resource Management, "Survey: 84 Percent of US Workers Blame Bad Managers for Creating Unnecessary Stress," August 12, 2020, https://www.shrm.org/about/press-room/survey-84-percent-u-s-workers-blame-bad-managers-creating-unnecessary-stress.

2. AceNgage, "Why 57% of Employees Leave Because of Their Managers?" Pulse (blog), LinkedIn, April 12, 2024, https://www.linkedin.com/pulse/why-57-employees-leave-because-managers-tr3ic.

CONCLUSION

1. Whitney Johnson and Amy Humble, "To Take Care of Others, Start by Taking Care of Yourself," *Health and Behavioral Science* (blog), *Harvard Business Review*, April 28, 2020, https://hbr.org/2020/04/to-take-care-of-others-start-by-taking-care-of-yourself.

Top 15 Coaches In Boston In 2024

BY INFLUENCE DIGEST | APRIL 04, 2024

Nestled on the East Coast of the United States, Boston stands out as a city that fascinatingly blends history with modernity. Known for its pivotal role in the American Revolution, the city boasts historical sites like the Freedom Trail and the USS Constitution Museum, attracting millions of visitors each year. But Boston is much more than its history. It is a melting pot of cultures, home to a diverse and multicultural population that contributes to its rich tapestry. With a reputation for academic excellence, it is host to world-renowned institutions like Harvard University and the Massachusetts Institute of Technology (MIT), drawing students and scholars from around the globe. This unique blend of history, culture, and knowledge creates an ideal environment for personal and professional growth. Coaches in Boston, aware of this richness, strive to help individuals and organizations reach their full potential in an environment that values excellence and continuous learning. In this article, we will explore some of the top coaches in Boston in 2024, highlighting their impact on the community and their ability to inspire and guide others toward success. So, without further delay, here are the Top 15 Coaches In Boston in 2024 that you can contact right now:

Chris Mader

Chris Mader, with nearly 3 decades of experience in revenue generation and talent development, founded MTA to help leaders achieve exceptional results. As a former athlete and Chief Revenue Officer, he has a unique perspective on performance and motivation.

He offers coaching, corporate training, and motivational speaking, and has developed leaders at all levels. His mission is to empower individuals and teams to reach their full potential while creating a positive workplace culture. MTA Consultancy supports companies' missions to increase revenue and improve employee engagement through a proven approach to identifying and developing talent.

Visit Chris' LinkedIn profile to learn more about how he can assist you.

Chris Mader
MTA Consultancy
April 2024

www.ingramcontent.com/pod-product-compliance
Lightning Source LLC
Chambersburg PA
CBHW070858160726
48004CB00003B/1136